Reverend Jen's
Les Misrahi

Reverend Jen's
Les Misrahi

Printed Matter, Inc.

Photo: Maurice Narcis

Les Misrahi
An Introduction

Les Misrahi is an entirely new art form – a satirical epic puppet show musical. While the presence of a sixty page puppet show in this book might seem to some to be a warning sign of my slowly-corroding mental state, my reasons for writing this gargantuan piece of puppet theater are numerous. For starters, puppet shows are often seen as harmless pieces of lighthearted theater. They rarely feature sex, violence, drug use and a token golden shower scene. But, I wanted to change all that. I wanted to write a puppet show that kicked ass, and so I did.

Secondly, I would like to perform *Les Misrahi* as an actual musical with human actors, but due to my current state of financial ruin, this is impossible for the time being, so instead I have made little puppets out of poster board, marker and Popsicle sticks, and built a puppet theater out of an old cardboard box. While this might not be the most visually stunning production in all the land, it is extremely low cost and more importantly, it properly communicates the feeling which inspired me to write this—a feeling of powerlessness, like being a child stuck in a world where it has no control over anything that happens around it and so it turns to its imagination. Perhaps it even writes a puppet show to express its secret rage wherein it paints a heinously unflattering portrait of the adults who it believes are ruining its life. When I was an adolescent I often used troll dolls and Barbies and puppets to express my disdain for the outside world. I clearly remember in the 4th or 5th grade performing a puppet show in front of my class, (which I wrote) about the genocide committed against the Native Americans by the white settlers. I wrote and performed it with the intention of writing a "serious" tragedy, but my manner of performing it was so ludicrous that all my classmates could do was laugh. I could only hold two puppets at once because I was also holding the script and so I kept dropping them on the ground. It was so pathetic that it was funny. Later I went into the bathroom and cried because I thought I had failed, but what I realize now is that it was an unforgettable performance. It was so outlandish and failed in such an extreme way that it was a great piece of theater. My manner of performing it, my confusion and my devotion to realizing the piece despite my total lack of puppetry and memorization skills was just as engaging as slick theater and this I suppose ultimately became my aesthetic.

Thirdly, I wrote *Les Misrahi* with the intention of satirizing my landlord who is notorious. Of course, I have magnified his negative traits tenfold, and have also created other characters based on people who I consider assholes and magnified their negative traits tenfold as well. If one were to liken *Les Misrahi* to *The Divine Comedy*, it is sort of like Dante taking all the people he thought were assholes and putting them in hell. (Just one of the obvious similarities!)

Finally, it is important that if one is to properly perform *Les Misrahi*, one must perform it directly in front of one's landlord's office, thus *Les Misrahi* could become an effective weapon against gentrification. When the models, TV producers and stockbrokers come to your landlord looking for 2,000 dollar a month studios, they will be forced to think twice when they see that your landlord's tenants are so embittered against him that they have taken to performing puppet shows about him in front of his office.

It is my hope that anyone who has ever been screwed over by a slumlord will take up arms, build a puppet theater, and go to their landlord's office where they will perform this piece of theater.

This puppet show is a work of fiction. Names, places, and incidents either are the products of the author's imagination or are used fictitiously. Any resemblance to actual persons, living or dead, or events or locales is entirely coincidental.

Scene 1

JEN VALJEAN (SINGING):
Making license plates all day is not very gay, especially when they all look at me like I'm a freak!

Oh yes, I've tried to make friends, but I seem to offend everyone who comes my way.

Demanding cigarette cartons, the others are so heartless, and I am so alone.

It's not like in the movies, when women in prison looked so groovy.

There's just no style in these threads,

No fancy sheets upon the beds,

And the stench of urine is EVERYWHERE!

To be a prisoner is not to be a winner, and everyday I grow thinner, living in this cage…

BURLY FEMALE PRISONER #1:
Hey Pixie Stick, how'd you like to lick my beef curtains? Is it true what they say about elves? They like to touch themselves!

BURLY FEMALE PRISONER #2:
Mmm, I sure would like a shot of elf juice to wash down my stale bread and water.

BURLY FEMALE PRISONER #3 (*slithering up behind jen*):
Hey, sweet cheeks, I made me a nice new dildo out of some scraps of rusty metal! Now if you toss me a fresh pack of cigs, I won't have to try it out on you!

JEN VALJEAN:
Please, no! I have no cigs, I swear to ya.

BURLY FEMALE PRISONER #3:
Why don't I just strip search you!

Prisoner #3 puts Jen in a chokehold, and she thrashes about. The attack is interrupted by Odius, a female prison guard.

ODIUS:
All right, you damn carpet-munchers, put yer vaginas away and listen up! I'm lookin' for prisoner #12127435, Saint Reverend Jen Valjean.

JEN VALJEAN:
Why, that's me. Am I free to go?

ODIUS:
You may go. But, you are not free. You are on parole, you stinking hole. And you must wear this golden 'T' upon your shirt, to let the peoples know you are a thieving pile of dirt.

JEN VALJEAN:
But all I did was steal a glue stick from the Houston Street Kinkos.

ODIUS:
It's because of you, you commie pinkos that the state is in decay.

JEN VALJEAN:
But, I have done my time. I have paid.

ODIUS:
Four years is nothing for the pain you have inflicted.

JEN VALJEAN:
Four years was too much! It was vindictive.

ODIUS:
You stole from an honest corporation. Now get the hell out before I smash your face in!

JEN VALJEAN:
You'll see, Odius, you'll see. I will make a new life for myself. I will become a brand new elf!

ODIUS:
Yeah, good luck to you, scum of the Earth. I wouldn't count on finding a soul on Earth, who will befriend you with that 'T' on your tit.

JEN VALJEAN:
Odius, just you wait. I'll be a big hit!

Scene 2

JEN VALJEAN:
Aha! Freedom is mine. The air it smells like ass! The sunlight is so fine! The people move so fast! Brick tenements and glittering cement! A pizza place is near! A place to get a beer! A slice it looks so tempting, but my pockets are so empty. I need to find employment before I seek enjoyment. My stomach it rumbles like a sym-

phony. Oh, Kinkos, unnumbered are the toils I bear because of thee. Hunger has already enslaved me, but already I see a chorus of rats approaching!

RAT CHORUS:
We heard tales of your suffering, Saint Reverend Jen Valjean, but don't give up. Embrace the dawn. Our people know hardship all too well. Onto many glue traps our loved ones fell. Cubes of cheese like sirens beckoned them, and so they were slain by the deception of men. Do not fall prey to such evil trickery! Though we rats are hardly niggardly, we haven't much to give to a starving elf, but please take these treats and take care of your self.

JEN VALJEAN:
A can of Budweiser! How very kind of you!

CHORUS OF RATS:
It is skunked, but it's the least we could do.

JEN VALJEAN:
Skunked or not. It will give me energy. The carbohydrates in beer will certainly fuel me. And, a blue pop tart! You rats are so generous. How did you obtain the reputation of being so lecherous?

CHORUS OF RATS:
It's because we are dirty, like you, that humans abandoned us. If we were cleaner like squirrels, there wouldn't be such a fuss.

JEN VALJEAN:
How, dear vermin can I ever repay you?

CHORUS OF RATS:
When the time comes you will know what to do. There is a great oracle on the Lower East Side that you will lead a revolution for the Downtrodden and Tired. All we ask is that you don't forget us. Our army of rats will take up arms for you, but there is no rush. Relax for now, and when the time comes, you will know when to fight!

JEN VALJEAN:
Me? A fighter? There is no might here. I am a weakling; done in by poverty, alone in rags I tell my sob story. This oracle—it must be wrong!

CHORUS OF RATS:
It is written in a song on the bathroom wall of Luna Lounge—that an elf in a tattered gown will battle hypocrisy and greed with an army of misfits whom she will lead. The bathroom wall is never

erroneous, often misspelled, but never full of bologna. Goodbye Saint Reverend Jen Valjean. Remember all we have told you and when the time comes, we will be there by your side. For now, take care of yourself. Take it in stride. Find a job. Fate alone won't feed your gob.

JEN VALJEAN:
Me—a chosen one! I can hardly believe. I am sort of like Jesus only not a hippy! Who do I kid? I can't let this go to my head! Jesus—yeah right! I'm an unemployed loser who knows not wrong from right. The rats were probably teasing—dishing up lies I found pleasing. Picking on humans as they often do—but I do need a job—that much is true.

What shall I do to earn my keep—temping seems quite sweet—Oh look—an agency! It is so very fancy.

Hallo, may I apply.

BOSS:
You don't know how to type! You don't know how to type!

JEN VALJEAN:
I promise I will try!

BOSS:
A thief like you means trouble! Better leave on the double.

JEN VALJEAN:
But all I stole's a glue stick.

BOSS:
You must think me thick. First a glue stick then a pen, then Xeroxes, then a desk. First one pencil then a hundred and ten. You'll steal what I don't glue down. Do you think I am a clown? Scram you lousy louse.

JEN VALJEAN:
But I don't even have a house!

Where on Earth will I live? What will I eat? I will surely starve upon the street. What's this a Village Voice?

Whatever is the price?

It is free I can afford it.

Help Wanted page 42—looking for a good girl like you,

Blonde, brunette or redhead.

Easy work. Easy bread.

I can do that. I have brown hair.

I shall hop the subway there.

Hallo, boss. I need a job.

BOSS:
You? You are a dirty slob.

JEN VALJEAN:
But, I saw it in the Voice. You need a good girl, like me.

BOSS:
Not an urchin who smells like pee. Not a criminal who wears a "T." You must be joking? What are you smoking? Crack must be your drug of choice you look so thin and pale. No man will lie with the likes of you—a convict from the jail.

JEN VALJEAN:
Oh, please, please, please, please, please.

BOSS:
Take a bath. You are covered in grease. Put on some rouge and some brand new clothes, then maybe I'll hire you as one of my hos.

JEN VALJEAN:
I am not even good enough to be a whore. What is it that I'm living for? Oh look—a clothing store! One more try can't hurt. Surely, I can sell a shirt.

Hallo, sir. Do you need a sales associate?

BOSS:
You, you smell like shit. I ain't gonna let no thief touch my outfits. You'd be better off scrubbing toilets.

JEN VALJEAN:
Sorry I asked, but please spare me the insults. Don't we all have our faults? What's this upon the lamppost that I see—dog walkers needed ASAP! Dog walker, cat sitter, that is me! I love those critters. They are nice. They won't care that I'm dirty and that I have lice.

Hallo, Boss, what do you think of me? Can I have a job with your company?

BOSS:
Me, I find you disgusting, but I have no time to be fussy. We've got a hundred dogs to walk and no one to walk 'em. Our other dog walker died of exhaustion. And, you, the dogs will love you for you are like them. You are dirty and stupid. You'll fit right in.

JEN VALJEAN:
Thank you! Thank you! I am ever so grateful despite the fact that

your opinions so hateful. When sir, can I start my new career?

BOSS:
You start today. Just grab the newspaper and leash I have here, and go across town to meet a golden retriever, your very first hound. Here is the address. Don't be tardy. Even a dog's bladder isn't so hearty.

Scene Three

JEN VALJEAN:
What is your name you friendly beast?

GOLDEN RETRIEVER:
Woof, woof, woof!

JEN VALJEAN:
OK, then I shall call you Steve. What's that Steve? Yes the world is cruel, and I am lucky to have a friend like you. You are so quiet and so nice. You seem content just to roll in the light. You don't insult me like those wicked humans do. You don't care that I smell like poo. You are soft and gentle and void of spite. You don't go looking for a fight. You just want to sniff and smell and pee. You just want to chase squirrels up a tree. You wag your tail as if to say, "Hi, friend." You've always got an ear to lend. Oh, I know you can't talk, but it's as if when we walk, you are listening and sympathizing. You are kind, and never criticizing! You know what Steve—I think I smell a song!

> Dogs are Nice
>
> Unlike humans.
>
> Dogs are nice
>
> Unlike people.
>
> Dogs are smart.
>
> Humans are feeble.
>
> Dogs are cool.
>
> People are not.
>
> Dogs like to play in the sunshine.
>
> Humans make war all the time.
>
> Dogs like to poop and to pee.
>
> Humans exploit humans overseas.

Dogs wag their tails.

Humans wave their fingers.

Dogs growl for food.

Humans pull the trigger.

Dogs hump chairs.

Human priests molest children.

Dogs dig holes that they bury sticks in.

Humans build multinational corporations, which cause massive global misery.

Dogs like to play with balls and Frisbees.

Humans like to play with each other's minds.

When dogs are happy, they wag their behinds.

Dogs are nice, unlike people.

Dogs are cool.

Humans are not.

I like dogs.

Woof, woof, woof…

Dogs are fun.

Woof, woof, woof.

Boy, Steve this is the best job I ever had. No lame stories at the water cooler. No bosses getting mad. So, I've gotta pick up a little poop. It's worth it for a friend like you. Say, it's getting late, and at 5 I've got a date, with a Chihuahua on Avenue A. First, I'll drop you at your address. My friend, you are the best!

Here I am at the Chihuhua's habitat. Oh my! It's as small as rat. Hallo, little fellow!

CHIHUAHUA:
Woof, woof, woof, woof, woof, woof, woof!

JEN VALJEAN:
My, my, you aren't too mellow. But, I like you well enough, for a tiny thing you are quite tough. What is your name little one? I shall call you Saint Reverend Jen Valjean the 2nd one, for like me, you've got pointed ears, with which to hear. You look just like a shrunken deer.

CHIHUAHUA:
Woof, woof, woof!

JEN VALJEAN:
I see that you approve. Now let us move. We've got walking to do. Shall I take you to the dog run, mini Reverend Jen Valjean? Off to Tompkins Square Park, it is still before dark. The cops won't be out yet. We are still free citizens. Aha—what a glorious sight to behold—a gaggle of mutts on the ground doth roll! Off you go petite creature—into a see of drool and fur! I shall protect you if bigger dogs think you're food. Ah—watch them play, so free and glorious. They seize the day.

Lights fade out and then fade back up again quickly.

JEN VALJEAN:
Hallo, Boss. I've worked twenty hours and need to get paid.

BOSS:
Here you go kid. Hope you don't mind rolling pennies.

JEN VALJEAN:
But Sir, this is only half the amount you promised me.

BOSS:
And, who are you to complain, you no good thief?

JEN VALJEAN:
But, but…

BOSS:
Go cry yourself to sleep, you elf eared freak!

JEN VALJEAN:
If only I had a pillow to cry on! If only I had a bed to dream on. My bitter tears freeze in the wind as I sleep outdoors behind a trash bin. At least my paltry pay will be enough to find a place for the week, just a ceiling and somewhere to sleep. I look to the lamppost for direction. What's this I detect? A crumpled flyer covered in scum. Chain smoking carnivore seeks someone to share a shit hole on Ludlow Street. The rent is cheap, cheap, cheap! The walls are covered in piss. The halls smells like vomit, but with the right touch, it could have some class to it. My tender loving care is all it needs! I'll paint the walls, and like Rhoda, I'll hang up beads. Martha Stewart look out. I've got my work cut out.

Scene 4

JEN VALJEAN:
112 Ludlow Street, buzzer eight, Hi, it's me. I've come about the place.

LARRONDO:
It's ten flights up at the top of the staircase. Before you come up, can you pick me up a pack of cigs—ultra lights, I'm trying to quit.

JEN VALJEAN:
Sure thing—what is your name?

LARRONDO:
Larrondo Newmane, you must be the homeless elf, Saint Reverend Jen Valjean.

JEN VALJEAN:
That is me. I need a room in which to stay.

LARRONDO:
Look no further. As long as you're not a famous mass murderer, you can move in as soon as this evening, just bring me those cigs—goddamnit, I'm jonesing!

JEN VALJEAN:
Here you go, fresh from the bodega.

LARRONDO:
Thanks little elf. What do I owe ya?

JEN VALJEAN:
Twenty-two dollars, with tax thirty-eight.

LARRONDO:
I'd be better off doing cocaine. Welcome new roommie. Make yourself comfy. As well as you can in this great big dump here. My landlord's a douche named Leon Misrahi. He drives a Mercedes while we live in poverty. Not his fault though. There's always rich and poor, I'd shut up if he installed a door. A smoke alarm we haven't. Our kitchen floor is bent. The pipes they spew black water, and no one ever bothers to clean the stinkin' halls. But enough of my bitching, what is it that you do best, and why is it that you wear a 'T' upon your chest? Is that an ode to Laverne Diffozio of my fave rave show?

JEN VALJEAN:
I was branded for stealing from Kinkos—a simple glue stick.

LARRONDO:
Oh dude—I hate those dicks!

JEN VALJEAN:
Four years I did at the women's penitentiary.

LARRONDO:
Sounds rather scary.

JEN VALJEAN:
This place is Heaven in comparison. I have learned my lesson.

LARRONDO:
Yeah, never get caught. Steal from corporations but never mom and pop. At Kinkos and Kmart it's open season, but only steal if it's for a good reason. Why'd you steal the glue?

JEN VALJEAN:
It was for a zine I was trying to do.

LARRONDO:
Good for you. Good for you. Now what are your plans?

JEN VALJEAN:
To keep my job and start a band. To write a book and learn to cook. To meet a love descended from above.

LARRONDO:
Yeah. He'd have to be descended from the skies, cause you're not gonna find him on the Lower East Side. Now listen up, dear. I've no intention of being mean, but I'm a bitter old queen, and I can tell you a couple of things about dudes.

South of Houston Street they're all alike, riding 'round on rickety bikes. Never working, always jerking the ladies around. You think you've found a good one, then he refuses to wear a condom. You think you've found a charmer, then he asks to call his partner. Dudes. *(Starts singing.)*

> Dudes
>
> Dudes down here aggravate me.
>
> Pot heads and attitude queens.
>
> Brown belts and black shoes.
>
> It's enough to make me lose my libido.
>
> Down here, dudes blow (and not in a good way) if you know,
>
> what I mean.

They think their cocks are made of gold.
They just need to be told,
That we can do better.
So don't hold your breath.
You might die an early death,
If you wait that long.
There are no Mister Rights in bohemian paradise,
Just a bunch of fuckin' lousy slackers.
Why, it's a known fact here,
None of 'em have jobs,
and none of 'em have ethics.
Here's another method: wash your face. Do your hair up.
Hop the bus to Tribeca.
Find a lawyer to protect you, and become his wife.
Get that ring on your finger.
But, don't you linger,
On thoughts of love
There are bigger goals in life.
Write your book.
Start your band,
but if you're lookin' for a man,
don't look here.
At the Boiler Room each night, I see a thousand Mr. Rights,
Ripped abs, fine pecs—you know they only last a night,
And then they're gone.
A glory hole is much better,
Than the dudes who tend to gather in this neck of the woods.
Straight or gay, it doesn't matter, though I prefer the later,
What your inclination.
Look elsewhere in the nation, for a dude.
Look, honey, we're both Queens,
And until dudes find the means for recognizing this,
Not a solitary kiss will be planted on their lips from this here mouth.
So, do yourself a favor, get a sturdy vibrator and stay in your room.

JEN VALJEAN:
Larrondo, you must have had your heart broken once to be so full of mistrust.

LARRONDO:
Ah—it's a long story, too long to tell and my eyes are glazed over like a lazy stoner's, and I feel the need to sleep. Why don't you stay? Put your stuff in a heap in that room, we'll get to know each other soon, but first may I ask you something? I'm sure it's nothing, but why are your ears so pointed? Are you really an elf?

JEN VALJEAN:
That very thing I have asked myself time and time again. I never knew my parents and this only brings me pain. I do not know from whence I come—born by a Queen or by a bum, I was but an orphan, although one thing is certain, my ears reach out to the celestial Heaven. I may not be immortal, but I am certainly not normal. Perhaps magic lurks inside me of the elvin variety, but my heart breaks just like another's. My tongue gets tied my lips, they stutter. I am weak, but strong because I never bite my tongue. I speak of the savage ways of our oppressors. I don't mean to depress ya, but this world of ours is fucked and we are almost out of luck, and because I am fond of you, my dear, dear Larrondo, I must tell you, the rats told me of a prophecy, and it could get quite messy, if I continue to stay. Now perhaps, the rats they jest me, but I must say, this legend, it tells of an elf who helps the poor to help themselves to a great big serving of what they've been needing. The tips of my ears pull me toward the stars, glistening in the night, but my heart tells me I must fight. I am so very tired, and do not know if this is true. I know only my desire for sleep and food. Tomorrow will show me, whether this rat-told prophecy holds any bearing on reality—but already, the desire churns inside me. The desire to do more than work 9 to 5; to punch a clock to watch life. I want to shake things up—to go out there and disrupt the way the wheels are turning, the sadness all around me.

LARRONDO:
You are an authentic elf, I'll have you know—a kindly creature, not a foe. I met one once in South New Jersey, playing the flute under a tree. It was so ethereal in its ways—an airy being who loved to play, but one whose wisdom told of days of affliction—of thousands of years to build up conviction, both wise and playful. It's heart and head were full of both mischief and good, and you, are very much like that being who airily floated beneath that tree. Now, many a fairy, I have met, but an elf—why they are of a separate mindset. The fairies, they do love to dance, to celebrate, and work a trance over any simple farmer, but the elves they are full of thought, of pondering eyes and wandering mind. Their joy is offset by concern

for all the creatures upon the Earth. It must be true! There's an elf sharing my room!

JEN VALJEAN:
And what of you, Larrondo Newmane, what's your deal? How is it that you get your meals?

LARRONDO:
I am a comic, a comedian. I get my dollars telling jokes to men who often heckle, and throw beer bottles. Once I was even throttled upon the stage by a drunk in a rage down in Kentucky, but with any luck I'll be famous in a month or two. Unemployment I'm collecting, and each day I'm waiting for the day when my ship comes in! Telling jokes ain't so easy, you try to appease the biggest asses in all the land. I'm a modern day jester, a clown without a costume, but I know someday that soon, NBC's gonna wake up, and the bidding wars they will erupt. Someday, I'll have a sitcom, called "The Larrondo Show with Larrondo Newmane." And, then, and only then I'll know the true taste of fame. But, now true elf, get some rest, already I have asked too much. In your time here, I wish you luck.

JEN VALJEAN:
Good night Larrondo Newmane. Let's call it a day.

LARRONDO:
Goodnight elf child. Sleep tight for the while.

Scene 5

JEN VALJEAN:
What is that banging that I hear? Someone at the door, their knock fills me with fear. Who is it there?

LEON:
It's Leon Misrahi, do you know what brought me?

JEN VALJEAN:
Like the sphinx, your riddles baffle. What is it sir? What is the hassle?

LEON:
Tell that dirt bag, Newmane that I've come for the rent again!

JEN VALJEAN:
Why, I'm sorry sir. Today he auditioned for Budweiser. Isn't that exciting?

LEON:
I hope the fag gets struck by lightning.

JEN VALJEAN:
I can assure you sir that we have the rent, only I'm afraid I'll have to post date the check.

LEON:
What kind of fool do you think I am? Do you think this is a squatt for you and your friends?

JEN VALJEAN:
If my friends are the roaches then that is the case. They have certainly made a home of the place. I suppose you should ask them for rent. I think the ones over there have pitched a tent.

LEON:
Listen you smart-assed imp, tell that faggot assed wimp, that if he doesn't pay, he'll certainly limp. I've got a whole posse who'd love to pop him in the knees. And, don't think you're immune! I haven't decided what I'll do. Perhaps I'll pull a "Van Gogh" if you know what I mean. You wouldn't look so keen missing an oversized listener!

JEN VALJEAN:
Now you listen here mister. I don't think you're very nice. We'll have your goddamn rent if I have to steal every damn cent from your snot-nosed neighbors out in good old Westchester.

LEON:
Aha! The 'T' on your chest! You're no better than the insect pests who share your abode—a roach you are—the lowest of the low. But, lucky for you, beneath that dirt, there is a pretty face. You just might be able to stay in this place. If you took a shower, you might have some power over my softer side. You've got such innocent eyes, such supple thighs. I've never had an elf before. Why don't you lock the door? I'll shave a couple dollars off your rent.

JEN VALJEAN:
You, sir are a miscreant. Not only that, you are married. Lay a hand on me and I'll see that you're buried before sunset.

LEON:
No need to fret. Just a little harmless flirtation, please don't lose patience with me. Just one little kiss, or are you a tease?

JEN VALJEAN:
I would rather screw a swarm of fleas. I would rather lick the ball sac of a dirty gnu than lay a hand on you. I would rather fuck ten

barnyard animals than cater to you filthy cannibals.

LEON:
Your words, they're getting me excited. Your demeanor is so feisty, not like my wife Mimi. She is such a bore, a fur-wearing, gold-digging whore. But, let me ask you, your gutter mouth did you get it in prison in between screwing bull-dyke lesbians? That must be it! You reject me because you play for the other team! If I had a vagina you'd be ready to please! Come here you little carpet muncher!

JEN VALJEAN:
Get out or you're going under!

LEON:
You don't know what you're missing. I could be the best thing you ever had. Like all lesbians, you are mad.

JEN VALJEAN:
Though I am no lesbian, I'd rather lick the clit of Andrea Dwarkin than caress your snake-like flesh.

LEON:
You are far too fresh. You'll see that your will won't last long. You'll see—once you can't afford to fill your bong that even that very precious skin of yours has a fee, then you'll come running to me.

JEN VALJEAN:
Don't count on it Misrahi, unless you want me to call up Mimi, or maybe I should call up the Post, I am sure they would find this most intriguing news.

LEON:
Just you try it, you flooze. The rent is due in one week. If I don't see green you'll see the street.

Scene Six

MIMI:
The spring it is approaching, but the snow is still around me. Good thing I've got my fur, made from the rarest cat in the world. Cost Leon 200 grand, had it shipped from across the land. Don't I look like a costly kitty, a diamond on this mucky street? Of course, I have several other furs, which I rotate on a weekly basis but out of them all this is my favorite.

BUM:
Hey lady, can you spare a dime or three.

MIMI:
Go back to OTB you walking STD! Yuck! The poor are so ill mannered, interfering in my daily agenda. Already I've forgotten. Have to check the palm pilot—ah, yes—at 2 I've got my botox injection, at 4 I've got my ladies luncheon, at 6 I've got my manicure—I have no time for the poor! How does Leon deal with those people? They are so dirty and so feeble. Yes, I know what they say about my husband, that he is a thug of a man. But, he's a landlord, not a welfare foundation. They don't know the hours he puts in, listening to them gripe and complain! The pipes are leaking! The rats are back again. So what? Sure it's no Home and Garden, but to them my heart is hardened. They should find better jobs—the filthy drunken slobs!

I know they say my hubby is a cheat—that he's dishonest—so he never wrote me sonnets—he's always got a kinder gift, the kind with Benjamin's face on it. Poetry won't keep you warm. There's no glamour to pen and ink, when compared with a brand new mink!

What's that ahead? Some dirty mongrels, they appear to be working on a mural. That's all we need, more stupid paintings about our oh so lovely community. In their hands they hold giant buckets, their hair is unwashed, their clothes are crumpled. The dirty hippies, I can smell them from here. I wonder what they want from me? Maybe a new razor to shave off those miles of armpit hair. What's that they wear on their jackets? An abbreviation of some manner, and in their free hands they hold a large banner. P.E.T.A.—I wonder what could it stand for? Puke eating, trashy assholes? Putrid, evil, terrible animals? Must be some punk rock slogan they use to piss off their parents whose homes they freeload in.

P.E.T.A. WORKER:
Come hear miss. I've something to tell you.

MIMI:
I have no money and I have no food. Go back to the forest from which you came!

P.E.T.A. WORKER:
I will take the blame. I will go to jail. This bitch deserves the whole pail. Onto her coat, I fling my red paint. Picasso I ain't, but it sure satisfies me to see her stand there crying. Her mascara running onto her Versace clothing. A beautiful cat died to keep this filth warm. It surely is disgusting. I am sorry it died in vain.

MIMI:
You ruined my coat, and now you start to gloat. You think it's funny! Do you know what Leon paid for me to wear such a gem?

P.E.T.A. WORKER:
I know what the animal paid! It's entire existence, snuffed out because of your material excess. It's barely under 50 degrees, you didn't need that thing anyway!

MIMI:
I have poor circulation. I have a thin epidermal.

P.E.T.A.. WORKER:
Buy some stinking thermals!

MIMI:
You people are sick. You've pushed me to the brink! When Leon is through with you, you won't be holding buckets, but the bars in your cell. The whole lot of you are going to hell! You can have my coat! It's not like anyone can clean it, and I have several others at home in my walk in closet. Here! Take that—I'd rather freeze than wear something soiled by a filthy hippy.

P.E.T.A. WORKER:
Why, thank you. We will give it to the homeless. I am sure they'll appreciate this.

MIMI:
The thought disgusts me. I don't know how you scumbags sleep!

P.E.T.A. WORKER:
Goodbye, and thank you for your charitable contribution.

MIMI:
Just wait. I'll get my retribution!

Scene Seven

JEN VALJEAN:
Walking dogs for fifteen hours is no delight. I love the critters, but, ouch—my thighs. My calves are weak, my feet are spent, but luckily, I've earned my rent. So close to home and yet so far away, I've ten more blocks till I can call it a day. A dish of spaghetti and my bed await! I am so cold, my hands are like ice cubes, my elf ears they burn, my stomach cries for food. A sorry sight am I, trudging home late at night. Oh look a group of school kids, making angels in the snow, so full of life so full of hope. Their parents must have cared to outfit them so well, new mittens and hats. It is easy to tell

someone loves them. But, here I am, not a cent to spend, so I wear what I have, all at once, layers of rags and no hat, on my body there is no fat to keep everything warm. I am a wilted form. My head it swoons. I cannot concentrate. I find it hard to pull my weight.

SCHOOL KID:
Hey you guys, look at that freak! Hey elf-girl, do you know how to speak? Or do you babble in some elvin tongue? If I was you, I'd start to run.

OTHER SCHOOL KID:
Yeah. We got a cache of snowballs in our igloo, just waitin' for someone like you!

JEN VALJEAN:
Please children, leave me alone. I am just trying to get home.

SCHOOL KID:
Oh my God, it can talk. It is a monster after all. Hey look out monster, here comes a snow ball!

JEN VALJEAN:
Ha ha! You missed. You throw like a lass. You belong in a sewing class.

OTHER SCHOOL KID:
That does it! This time I'm aiming for your cranium. And, I won't miss, you can bet your bum.

JEN VALJEAN:
Ouch! He has hit me in the head with an icy snowball. The impact is causing me to fall. Onto a mound of snow, I find myself collapsing, my mind it is lapsing into a sleeping state.

SCHOOL KID:
Oh shit, I think we killed it, let's not waste another minute on this street. Pretty soon, the cops'll be walkin' the beat. We're not goin' to jail for killing no elf. We've gotta look after ourselves!

OTHER SCHOOL KID:
You're right. Let's scram on the double. I don't want any trouble. Someone will find her and bury her proper, but I ain't talking to no damn copper.

SCHOOL KID:
Yeah, and it's a Friday night. In an hour or two the streets will come to life. All the frat boys will be partying, look I see a few of them fast approaching. Let's go before they see us!

FRAT BOY #1:
Man I have to piss! Been drinkin' all night on Avenue A, my bladder's in an awful way.

FRAT BOY #2:
Yeah man, I have to drain my lizard. I hope my piss doesn't freeze in the blizzard.

FRAT BOY #3:
Goddamn, I have to pee as well. Those two for ones at Coyote Ugly made my bladder swell.

FRAT BOY #4:
Damn, me too. Beer is for rent not for sale. Does anyone have a pale?

FRAT BOY #5:
I wish this fuckin' city had public toilets, and where's a McDonald's when you need it?

FRAT BOY #6:
I guess we're all going to have to whip out our dicks and drain our beer. That like doesn't make us queer?

FRAT BOY #1:
Of course not, let's get in a circle, around this patch of snow.

FRAT BOY #2:
Yeah, we're only doin' it cuz we gotta go. All right, now undo your zippers slow.

FRAT BOY #3:
Yeah, let 'em slip off your hips.

FRAT BOY #4:
Oops! I think your dick froze on my lips! How did that happen? I ain't no gay!

FRAT BOY #5:
Come on guys, let's piss today. The Boiler Room's around the corner then you can play.

FRAT BOY #3:
Ah! A hot stream of piss does escape me. I feel light. I feel free.

FRAT BOY #4:
The snow is yellow and black, like a bee.

FRAT BOY #2:
All this male bonding is getting me aroused. Let's go back to the Frat House.

FRAT BOY #1:
Golden Showers anyone?

FRAT BOY #5:
That sounds like good, clean fun!

FRAT BOY #6:
Wow, it sure feels good to let go! Holy shit what's that, in the snow?

FRAT BOY #3:
We pissed on an elf! Holy shit!

FRAT BOY #4:
Ah, elves are kinky. She probably liked it.

FRAT BOY #5:
Dudes, I think she's dead.

FRAT BOY #1:
Then she doesn't care that there's piss on her head. Come on, we have better things to do than fuckin' stand and watch some imp turn blue.

FRAT BOY #2:
Yeah, let's go. The next round is on me! It's time to Par-Tay!

Scene Eight

URISTAT:
Oh no! It's almost noon! The Cyclops, Solange, will be expecting me soon. But, so many errands it gives me and if I'm not back, it'll come looking. Its one eye sees everything. Go to Key Food for the grocery! Pick up my heaps of laundry! Do the dishes! They are dirty! And, only an hour I get in which to leave its cave. I Uristat, a slave, to the French Cyclops, Solange. Once I was its lover, but those days are gone. Years ago, it had the veneer of a beautiful woman, and I loved what lay on the surface. Intoxicated by her perfume, blinded by her hips. I failed to acknowledge her vile personality, but with her whiles, she managed to trap me. The monster, it had played a trick on me.

Late one night, as I held her ivory skin, I felt a change begin. I opened my eyes and began to vomit! It had turned into a one-eyed cretin! "So," it said, "You think I am a lady? It was so easy to play thee! I am no woman at all, but a monster scorned by the Gods."

"But, but," I stammered, "You were slain by Odysseus!"

"My child, that was only a myth!" it laughed! "I have been living in the South of France. I moved to New York when I got the chance. When you are immortal the world is very small."

"No, this can't be!"

"What's wrong? You no longer love me? I am no longer pretty, and so you don't want me? Do not worry, my gentle Uristat, you have no choice as to what you get. I have chosen you to be my lover, and my slave. You were so naïve, I couldn't resist!'"

"You deceived me. I am putting an end to this tryst."

"Try it, dear slave. The door is open."

I approached the door, and as I did, it shut in my face. I was completely disgraced. The Cyclops has powers beyond that of men. I am no match for its iron hands. I have tried to escape, but it always finds me, and I am forced to endure such misery. One hour a day is all I get to leave its cave, and when I return, I am forced to lay by its side; its skin like hide, its body odor like that of ten apes. I sit on the floor and crush its grapes to make its wine. I prepare its meals so that it may dine, but all I eat is stale bread so that it may be fed heaping servings of meat. I am so lonely for a kind heart to love me, but if I do the Cyclops will see out of its omniscient eye, and for that I'll surely have to pay my life.

It is better not to think on it. It makes me cry. It makes me sick.

There is something on the sidewalk ahead. It appears to be a body laid out for dead.

Oh my God! It is an elf, a beauteous creature of kindly features. Yellow icicles have formed around its hair. Its lips are blue in the chilly air yet it seems to be alive by a thread so bare. The wind chill factor must be one degree; it's a wonder it can still breathe. I am no Doctor what should I do? If I linger much longer, Solange will be furious, but I am so very curious. I have never talked to an elf, and if I were freezing, I would want the same for myself. How is it no one cares enough to save this deity from the rough. Perhaps, I should drape this colorful fur that was given to me around its elvin body. Even though it would never fit the Cyclops, I knew it would come in handy. Although, I hear furs are out this season, I love the red streak someone put in. A creative touch, it suits her face. Here elf-girl, don't die today. Now, what else—oh yes! I have a slice from Sal Rosario's. I'll put it in her mouth and see if she can chew. It seems to be adding color to her face, but her eyes they are closed as if she might waste away. Oh, I wish someone would come my way.

Hallo! Hallo! Can anyone help me? What's this? A group of bipedal rats have appeared!

CHORUS OF RATS:
Hallo, Uristat. You must do something, which will endanger your well being, but it will help the people of the future. This elf here is the leader mentioned in the Oracle.

URISTAT:
The famed oracle on the bathroom wall of Luna?

CHORUS OF RATS:
That is the one, but she will be dead soon, unless you move fast. You must kiss this elf on the lips.

URISTAT:
But, Solange, she will have me killed.

CHORUS OF RATS:
We will take care of the Cyclops. We know what to do. Now, do your part, get on top.

URISTAT:
Ok, ok. Do I slip her the tongue?

CHORUS OF RATS:
How should we know? We're rats, we don't know what you humans find fun.

URISTAT:
Here goes nothing. Yuck, she tastes like pee, but it is overshadowed by her fragile beauty.

CHORUS OF RATS:
Enough of your talking, you're not in the story to behave like a pussy boy!

URISTAT:
I press my lips hard upon hers, and it awakens in me a passion. I love her frozen lips and her long eyelashes. Suddenly, I have forgotten all about the Cyclops. This one kiss was worth it, if death be the cost.

CHORUS OF RATS:
You have done it Uristat! She is awake! Now we will leave the both of you to fate.

URISTAT:
But, the Cyclops, you said you would help me!

CHORUS OF RATS:
Don't go back to its cave whatever you do. When the time comes, we will protect you.

JEN VALJEAN (*waking up*):
Where am I?

URISTAT:
Tenth and A.

JEN VALJEAN:
Who are you?

URISTAT:
Someone who adores you. My name is Uristat.

JEN VALJEAN:
I have a feeling like I already knew that, like we've been separated for centuries and now we finally meet again. My name is Jen Valjean, but you may call me Jen.

URISTAT:
I should call you Gem for you shine like a diamond, and your manner of dress is truly outrageous. Your hair, though coated in piss fills my heart with bliss.

JEN VALJEAN:
And, you Uristat, are like an angel, your eyes speak of things celestial. I must be dead and in Heaven, or this is the trick of a juvenile delinquent.

URISTAT:
You were passed out on the sidewalk, seconds away from being an outline of chalk.

JEN VALJEAN:
What is today?

URISTAT:
The 15th of March.

JEN VALJEAN:
Aha! It's all coming back—the snowball; it made a whack, against my head. I should be dead! Kindly Uristat, you saved my life.

URISTAT:
With some help from your rodent friends.

JEN VALJEAN:
They've always got a hand to lend.

URISTAT:
They told me of the oracle, and now I'm in quite a debacle.

JEN VALJEAN:
Why is that dear Uristat?

URISTAT:
I have made the Cyclops mad.

JEN VALJEAN:
The Cyclops! Why, that is a fantasy!

URISTAT:
Like talking rats and elvin ladies?

JEN VALJEAN:
You have a point. Where is this Cyclops' joint?

URISTAT:
In a cave on Avenue D., where I was expected at half past three. I am her slave, for life she tells me, but the things that happened today have turned a new page. The Cyclops will be in a jealous rage.

JEN VALJEAN:
Why is that, Uristat?

URISTAT:
Your elvin lips, they touched mine bringing color to your face and light into your eyes. The rats, they told me I must kiss you, no doubt the Cyclops saw the whole scenario. Like a crystal ball, its eye sees me at every turn, but in my heart, a passion burns, to escape her and be with you.

JEN VALJEAN:
That means we must go soon! She must be on our trail. Our location she must see. Come Uristat, stay with me.

URISTAT:
That is very kind of you, but the danger I am in can only spell doom. I don't want you wrapped up in it. The Cyclops she will break my neck.

JEN VALJEAN:
My life is already a wreck. I am in danger all the time. Come, let's get a bottle of wine, and forget about her, until we have a plan. My

pockets are filled with cash. Fifteen hours I worked yesterday, so I can pay Misrahi. What's this? My pockets are empty! I was robbed while passed out on street!

URISTAT:
I will find whoever did that, and I will give them some of this and some of that!

JEN VALJEAN:
It's no use, Uristat. I must go home and pack. With no rent money to pay, I'll have to find a sturdy box today.

URISTAT:
In that case make it a box for two. I will not abandon you. If what the rats say is true, you have plenty of work to do.

JEN VALJEAN:
For the first time, I feel I'm not alone. The joy I feel outweighs the woe.

Scene Nine

JEN VALJEAN:
This is my place. It's not very pleasing although I'm sad to leave it.

URISTAT:
It sure is as cold as a witch's tit.

JEN VALJEAN:
My landlord's got a thing about the heat. He never turns it on that is; God—what a creep.

URISTAT:
Even in the middle of winter?

JEN VALJEAN:
Even in a blizzard. The boiler's covered in cobwebs, hasn't been touched in ages. I guess I'll break the news to poor Larrondo that now he'll have to pay rent for two or find a new roommate on the double. Wherever I go there's always trouble. Larrondo, are you here? Hello? Hello? That's funny, there's a half opened beer. I hear his TV. Let me check in his room and see. Oh my GOD, look in here!

URISTAT:
What is it dear? Oh my, your roommate is frozen into a block of

ice. His hand is on his crotch, frozen in static motion. Next to his bed there's a tube of lotion. On the TV plays a classic video—"Men who drink piss, volume 22."

JEN VALJEAN:
Never have I faced such a predicament. What should I do? Grab a chisel; we'll start to chip away until he's freed.

URISTAT:
Grab a blow dryer. I'll start a fire, and call up Mr. Misrahi.

JEN VALJEAN:
Hallo. Is this the landlord's office? I came home and noticed that my roommate is frozen in ice.

SECRETARY (V.O.):
An ice sculpture can be quite nice.

JEN VALJEAN:
Don't you understand—he is going to die!

SECRETARY (V.O.):
Not my department. By the way, where's the rent? You're ten days late. I guess this is his fate, good thing it got him before liver disease!

JEN VALJEAN:
You rotten sleaze, I'm calling the housing authority.

SECRETARY (V.O.):
Ooooh, I'm really worried. Bye, bye hon, have fun.

JEN VALJEAN:
Hallo, Housing Authority, I've got a complaint against Leon Misrahi.

OPERATOR (V.O.):
You've got lots of company.

JEN VALJEAN:
My roommate's encased in a giant ice cube.

OPERATOR (V.O.):
Look, whatever you're doing, just use lube. I've got no time for you kinky crank callers rambling on about your leather and collars. Asphyxiation and ice—I'm not into it, unless you wanna pay me five dollars a minute.

JEN VALJEAN:
Good God, I am not lying. There is no heat. My roommate is dying.

OPERATOR (V.O.):
I can send an inspector out, when through the week are you around?

JEN VALJEAN:
I work all week. I'm home at night.

OPERATOR (V.O.):
Sorry, can't help your fight. We have one inspector available, ten weeks from now at exactly 11 am. Will you be around then?

JEN VALJEAN:
It's no use!
(To be sung)

    My roommate is frozen into an ice cube,

    And there's nothing I can do.

    Once he was a living man—a slacker, but still a man.

URISTAT:
(Sung)

    Why, it's fact dear, the heat is scarce here,

    And outside there is a blizzard.

    And we are not lizards, cold-blooded creatures.

JEN VALJEAN:

    Our hearts are warm yet our bodies shiver

    The tears, which flow, they are quite bitter.

    The whiskey it rips at our livers,

    But we need to stay warm.

URISTAT:

    Your roommate has taken on a new form.

    He is a cube for a giant cocktail.

    We must try to melt him. We cannot fail.

JEN VALJEAN:

    The landlord has gone too far.

    This man was once an art star.

    And now he dies at a snail's pace.

    Through the ice I see his face,

    Turning blue, what oh what shall I do?

The Housing Authority you never see.
They are like Snuffelupagus;
A mystery to me.

URISTAT:
Misrahi has blood on his hands,
We will call a newspaper man.
When the people find out they will be outraged,
When they see this story on the front page.
Call them up!

NEWSPAPER RECEPTIONIST (V.O.):
Hallo, New York Chronicle, what's up?

JEN VALJEAN:
The rent I pay to that fiend Misrahi, but I called for I have a tragic story that needs telling.

NEWSPAPER RECEPTIONIST (V.O.):
We like tragic. It's good for selling. Tragic and gory; always good stories. What's your tale; is it front page fodder?

JEN VALJEAN:
It is hotter than any item, full of sorrow and pitiable creatures.

NEWSPAPER RECEPTIONIST (V.O.):
Sounds like a feature!

JEN VALJEAN:
My roommate, you see, use to be human like you and me,
But the lack of heat in our home transformed him
Into an ice cube, and my landlord says there is nothing he can do.
If he turned on the heat, it might melt the ice,
But he is too stingy to pay the price.

NEWSPAPER RECEPTIONIST (V.O.):
Who is this landlord of whom you speak?

JEN VALJEAN:
The rapscallion, Leon Misrahi.

NEWSPAPER RECEPTIONIST (V.O.):
Of him I have heard horrible stuff. You, my dear, have told me enough. Will you be at home? Can we send a photographer? This is

front-page fodder. You will be a star!

Scene Ten

LEON:
Oh secretary, can you bring me my morning coffee and my copy of the New York Chronicle?

SECRETARY:
Sir, I'm afraid there has been a debacle. This morning's paper you don't want to see, the contents are quite damaging.

LEON:
Oh, how bad can it be? Just bring me the paper sweet cheeks.

SECRETARY:
Whatever you say your majesty.

SECRETARY (*to herself*):
I'd like to put arsenic in your coffee you balding cretin. If you only knew the thoughts I'm keeping. To see your fat head lopped off would give me pleasure. The things the paper says here are nothing compared to your odious behavior. Get the coffee! Bring me the paper! Lift your skirt! Such a scumbag is bound to get his, and, I'll be laughing and filled with bliss when that day comes. Until then, I'll shine like the sun, pretending to be his faithful servant, collecting my meager pay, attempting to keep my sanity intact, smiling to hide my clenched fist until I get so pissed I slap his wrinkled face and get fired from this place.

SECRETARY:
Here you go sir, your coffee and your paper.

LEON:
What the hell is this crap you hand me? Man frozen because of Misrahi! Notorious slumlord Leon Misrahi, crossed a boundary, when he turned off the heat during a raging snowstorm! Oh boohoo! I never once turned it on! The press always gets it wrong. Struggling thirty-something gay comedian, Larrondo Newmane was discovered by his roommate, our sources say, frozen into a block of ice this past Thursday night. The bewildered roommate, Jen Valjean, attempted to free the young man's noggin by applying heat to the layers of ice. Indeed the poor pay a great price, living in such dire circumstances, doctors say the chances of Newmane's survival are slim. So that's

what happened to him! I was wondering where he'd been. I prefer him this way. They should freeze all the gays! Oh happy day! But, then again, this press is so negative. I'll have to do something about that little imp. Her with her pointed ears. I'll admit, I have my fears, if what the oracle says is true, my time is due to face the fact that I've been getting fat, while the others waste away. Soon, I will be forced to pay, but until then I shall live high on the hog. Who cares if it's wrong? Little miss elf ears can eat my ass. I've got money. I've got class (burps). What's that ruckus outside my window? Protesters gathered to let me know that I am no good. Hey you hippies—find a new neighborhood!

PROTESTORS:
You are a beast! You are a sleaze! Larrondo Newmane is frozen in ice. Until he is freed, we will fight!

LEON:
You think you're so smart with your hand made signs, you're no match for my designs. I've got one thing you don't; the boys in blue are on my side. I've got the muscle I've got the might. A plunger or two will keep you quiet.

PROTESTORS:
You may have money you may have thugs, but we won't sweep this under a rug. Call the cops. Take us to prison. We'll call the papers and they will listen.

LEON:
Hallo. Pitt Street Station, bring in the battalion. We've got a group of filthy protestors, blocking the sidewalk, making a nuisance.

COP:
We'll see how lively they are in prison.

LEON:
That's what I like to hear.

COP:
We'll squash this shit. Have no fear.

LEON:
Bring on the paddy wagon. Bring on the clubs; search their clothes, snag their drugs. We'll double the charge. Our profits will be rather large.

COP:
No problem sir as long as we keep our understanding. If you know what I mean.

LEON:
You want the cash. You want the green. Now get out there and stomp these freaks.

COP:
It will be my pleasure. Opportunities like these I certainly treasure. The Mayor will be happy I am sure.

LEON:
There's probably a promotion in it for you. Mayor McSleaze likes his jails to be full.

COP
His quotas are high, so that I am forced to ticket anyone who strays from the course of proper behavior. A lit weed stick or an open container will get you a year. We control the people through fear.

LEON:
As well you should. They are too stupid to amount to any good. And, they are not rich enough to break the rules. So get out there and do your duty. Come back and collect your booty.

COP:
All right, sleazebags, the brouhaha is terminated, pack up your signs. As the mayor has stated, you need a permit to assemble.

PROTESTOR:
Man—you're an asshole.

COP:
All right, you are going to jail.

PROTESTOR:
Freedom of speech; I can say what I please.

COP:
Tell that to Mayor McSleaze. He bought this city, fair and square! Hey is that a Marijuana cigarette I see over there?

PROTESTOR #2:
No sir it's tobacco.

COP:
Do you kids think I don't know what your doing? Taking drugs and fornicating. You should all be jailed and stripped of your civil liberties. You bunch of filthy fucking hippies.

PROTESTOR #3:
Fuck you pig!

COP:
That's it. A mistake so big will certainly cost you. Boys get your clubs. I've been accosted.

PROTESTOR:
No donut for you, you fuckin' nazi.

COP:
Now I'm really steamed. Get the cuffs. Arrest them all. This is great! What a ball.

Scene Eleven

URISTAT:
This growth light seems to be working. The ice appears to be melting. It was nice of the botanist to lend it to me.

JEN VALJEAN:
Fast Ricky is a good guy. Not only that his prices are right.

URISTAT:
I just wish we could get a doctor.

JEN VALJEAN:
Forget about it. We are too poor.

URISTAT:
Did you hear that? A knock at the door.

JEN VALJEAN:
Must be more neighbors bringing blow dryers. I'm amazed by all the support.

URISTAT:
Thank you neighbor. This is too kind.

NEIGHBOR:
It's all I could find. I hope you sue Misrahi's ass. What he did today was horribly crass.

JEN VALJEAN:
What did he do?

NEIGHBOR:
When the crowd arrived a fit he threw. Had them all arrested and beaten. The protestors, they were defeated. It's all over the news although it's severely twisted. Says the group had raised fists. In truth, they were peaceful, if not boring. But, the minute they showed up, the cops poured in. Lowering clubs and throwing punches, but I've got my hunches. Seems Misrahi must've paid them to do it.

JEN VALJEAN:
The lousy piece of shit! I've been so wrapped up in defrosting the roommie, the news I didn't see. Thanks for the update and the hairdryer.

NEIGHBOR:
No problem. We're gonna beat that liar. Just you wait and see.

URISTAT:
Goodbye kind neighbor.

NEIGHBOR:
Always happy to do a favor. Goodbye friend.

JEN VALJEAN:
Uristat, I am so glad to have your company.

URISTAT:
To be here with you is a delectable treat. Kiss me again with those elvin lips. Though you wear a 'T' on your tit, I know that you are good.

JEN VALJEAN:
You, Uristat, are like food, which nourishes a heart long broken.

URISTAT:
No words be spoken, I know everything you feel from your glances.

JEN VALJEAN:
My heart it leaps and dances like a child overjoyed. Ah, this is what romance is.

URISTAT:
And, now a kiss. Let those lips of yours linger as I slip my fingers under your tattered dress.

JEN VALJEAN:
I confess. It feels too good to be reality. Slip off my cotton panties

and fill me with your love.

URISTAT:
We will take it slow. I want to see your naked flesh glow. I want to give you the years of pleasure stolen from you in prison.

JEN VALJEAN:
The rusty dildos, the multiple fistings, they killed my passion years ago. This joy, I thought I would never know again.

URISTAT:
Saint Jen Valjean, I love you.

JEN VALJEAN:
And I love you. Dark days of abstinence are through. Take me Uristat. I am yours.

(Puppet Sex Scene. Special effects should be considered. "Kashmir" by Led Zeppelin should be played.)

URISTAT:
To lie here spooning you is all I ever want to do.

JEN VALJEAN:
You feel so good so warm and protecting, against my back I feel you growing.

URISTAT:
It can't be helped that I am popping wood, your elvin skin, it feels so good.

JEN VALJEAN:
How many hours have we been snuggled here? It feels like years that you've been holding me, and yet I have to get up and pee.

URISTAT:
Go ahead my love and drain your kitty. I will keep the bed warm for thee.

JEN VALJEAN:
Another knock at the door! Hand me my robe, must be a neighbor.

URISTAT:
Don't be too long!

JEN VALJEAN:
That knock is strong and impatient. Who is it?

SOLANGE (*in high voice*):
It's a friendly neighbor. I've come to melt the ice covered queer.

JEN VALJEAN:
How very kind of you. I shall open the door.

SOLANGE (*in monster voice, with French accent*):
You filthy whore! I have come to destroy you, elvin trash. You better think fast! I've brought my handy club, with which I shall bash your tiny head.

JEN VALJEAN:
I am filled with dread. Uristat come at once. I am a dunce. I should have never opened the door.

SOLANGE:
I shall kick you to the floor, and once I am sure that you are a goner, I will take my bat to your lover. Dearest Uristat, come save your elf before she feels the bat against her freckled flesh.

URISTAT:
What a mess! Solange, put down the club. I will do anything. I'll give you a back rub. I'll make you dinner, clean your cave; be your lover. Just don't harm Jen, that's all I ask.

SOLANGE:
Do you take me for a fool, Uristat? You will run away like you always do. Your time is up. You are through. I look forward to seeing the blood pour forth from your head, if you think you can lie in bed with another, I'll put you six feet under. This club is covered in spikes all the better to take your life. I swing my bat like Derek Jeter, it will make a good elf-meat tenderizer. One, two, three! I'm hungry for some elf meat.

JEN VALJEAN:
Oh no! A club to the head, I am falling. Perhaps I'm dead. Last words fail me. I fall into a deep sleep. Goodbye Uristat, I imagine that we will meet again.

URISTAT:
No! Gentle Jen Valjean. How dare you take the life of such a creature? You, you are a monster!

SOLANGE:
I like you better with her out of the picture. What do you say we go back to the cave?

URISTAT:
I would rather see the end of my days than spend another minute

with you. Without my elf, I am not my self, and I have lost my will to live. My life I will give if you are the alternative!

SOLANGE:
Very well then, I swing my bat, and hope to whack you where it smarts.

URISTAT:
You have already slain my heart. I stand before you dead already, waiting for you to numb me physically. It seems my friends, the rats, they failed me.

CHORUS OF RATS:
Sorry we are late. A starving loved one took the bait of cheese left out at night. The trap it clamped around him tight. It took our whole population to free his waist from the deadly vice.

URISTAT:
You have paid a dear price.

CHORUS OF RATS:
Our eyes, they water to look upon the slain elf. We were no help, but the oracle, it can't be wrong.

URISTAT:
But the Cyclops it is so strong.

SOLANGE:
What is this shit? Talking rats? Look, I came here to kick some ass, and I'm not leavin' till that's done. Look out Uristat, here it comes!

URISTAT:
The bat it lands on my ribs, yet I continue to live. Aim for my head and get it over with. Until I can lie in peace with Jen Valjean, I shall never smile again. Huddled over in pain I moan, yet this pain is nothing to the heart mowed down.

CHORUS OF RATS (*in a whisper to Uristat*):
Wait! The elf she is breathing. Her heart it is beating. Cyclops is a dirty fighter to maim this kindly sprite here. Uristat, take our lighter. Grab that pack of Larrondo's cigs, bundle 'em up like a bunch of twigs. Light 'em up till they're a flaming fire, then stick 'em in the Cyclops eye. Here!

URISTAT:
Seven cigs oughta do it. This is a good trick. The rats, they are smart, but I've got to deceive if I want to leave alive. How to get close to the eye?

URISTAT (*to Solange*):
Dear Solange, can't we compromise? I forgive you for smashing my ribs.

SOLANGE:
Rats, go back into your hole, and don't tell a soul what you saw me do. Uristat and I have business to attend to.

CHORUS OF RATS:
So long Uristat. We will creep away like lowly rats.

URISTAT:
Solange what you need is to relax. A cigarette will pacify you. I'll light up two, one for me and one for you. Come closer, and let me gaze, into that one eye so filled with rage. What is it that sets you off? Don't you have a side that's soft.

SOLANGE:
Your change of heart I find enticing, but there's plenty of slicing and dicing to be done. I'm going to have a meal of elf, and I certainly won't cook it by myself. You're still my slave, first and foremost.

URISTAT:
Is that so? Here take these cigs… in your eye!

SOLANGE:
I am blind! Woe is me. I am blind. Done in by my slave, a tricky knave. I wander in the darkness disoriented, swinging my bat looking for Uristat. Where are you selfish man after all I've done after all I still can? Didn't I treat you well as my servant? I deserved better treatment!

CHORUS OF RATS:
Heinous beast, you are under attack. You thought we were gone, but we are back. Uristat, tend to Jen, we will tend to this monster, like Splinter, we are ninjas. Take that vile creature!

SOLANGE:
Rat limbs punch my skin. Their tiny incisors pierce my flesh. Who knew their strength could be so great? I swing my bat in blind fury looking for anything small and furry. What's this? Something cold and wet, might as well take a crack at it!

URISTAT:
The ice it breaks! Larrondo is free.

LARRONDO:
Damn I have to pee. It wasn't bad enough I was trapped in fucking

ice. I had to watch you straight fuckers breeding. Gross! What the hell is that thing that's bleeding? Can you all get the hell out so I can finish my jacking?

URISTAT:
I am Uristat…

LARRONDO:
Yeah. I heard all about that. This ice is paper-thin. Open the cupboard; get me some tonic and gin. This is really too much for me to deal with. What the hell are those? Rats in togas. This gets weirder as the story grows.

CHORUS OF RATS:
We are Jen Valjean's protectors.

LARRONDO:
In that case, glad to meet ya!

SOLANGE:
Zut Alors! Someone kill me. I can no longer listen to his whining.

CHORUS OF RATS:
In a daze, she wanders onto the fire escape. Heave ho, heave ho, over the railing she will go.

SOLANGE:
I am falling like a giant, bruise covered snowflake. I know it is too late to save myself. Without my eye life would be hell. I am happy to go. I only wish I could've taken my foes down with me.

CHORUS OF RATS:
Splat out onto the street she lands, where pedestrians gaze in horror at her twisted limbs. What a mess she is. Now we must check on Jen.

URISTAT:
She is all right, with a slight concussion, her skull did not get bashed in.

CHORUS OF RATS:
Her skull is made of tough stuff. Let's put her to bed, she's had enough for one day. And, you, Uristat, are you in a bad way?

URISTAT:
My ribs, they are busted. I am glad I trusted you.

CHORUS OF RATS:
We have a doctor who knows mostly rat medicine, but he occasionally helps a person. We will have him look at you.

URISTAT:
Thanks dudes.

CHORUS OF RATS:
Jen, can you speak?

JEN VALJEAN:
My lips they are weary, but I hope you can hear me as I say 'thank you.'

CHORUS OF RATS:
It was almost simple to defeat such a dim-witted creature, and now you must get some ice for you. Here, put this on your head, and get to bed for tomorrow is another challenge.

JEN VALJEAN:
I was afraid that was the case.

JEN VALJEAN (*to self*):
Fast asleep I am falling, but my dreams, they are calling and instructing me. It is in this stupor that I see images of things to come. I see the scum subjugated. I see the people liberated. The rats, they dance through the air. People smile everywhere. The rent, it is close to nothing. Landlords, they are loving. Will this ever be our nation, or is this my imagination?

Scene Twelve

URISTAT:
Ah to wake up in the arms of a lover, without a hint of fear, we linger under the covers. Come dear…

JEN VALJEAN:
I had the strangest dream last night…there was a brutal fight.

URISTAT:
That was no dream. The rats made an excellent team. The Cyclops is dead. By the way, how's your head?

JEN VALJEAN:
There is bump the size of a cow.

URISTAT:
I love you anyhow.

JEN VALJEAN:
I would love to linger all day, but I still have my rent bill to pay, and the dogs they need me.

LARRONDO:
Wake up roommie, wake up! A photographer is coming up. We are all heroic stars. We'll get free drinks in all the bars! It's all over the headlines—Evil Cyclops dies in brutal fight. Gay comic freed from ice. Look at my picture! Do you think I look fat? Look at this, look at that! Channel Seven is coming at three, but look at me! I've got to comb my hair, look alive. New York One is coming at five. Micheal Musto is coming at 4:00. I feel like a media whore!

JEN VALJEAN:
You deserve it Larrondo, after all you've been through.

URISTAT:
It is all very exciting, but, what about Misrahi?

JEN VALJEAN:
How 'bout a massive rent strike? I mean, Larrondo almost died.

LARRONDO:
That's a good idea. We'll spread the word when the press comes around! I'll take that bastard down! In the mean time, do you have any powder? I don't want to look shiny when the press comes over!

Scene Thirteen

LEON:
So, miss elf ears and that queer think they can lounge around and not pay rent. I'll collect every cent if it's the last thing I do!

Aha, what's this outside my window, it's little Jen Valjean, walking a Chihuahua! I hope she doesn't think she can snub the "no pets" ordinance on the lease. I will steal that hairy beast, or even better, I steal its sweater. Nah—I'll do something better; I'll break its legs! Ha, ha, ha, ha, ha, ha!

JEN VALJEAN:
Jen Valjean Junior, you look so cute in your new sweater. I am so glad to be back at my occupation after Solange bashed my head in. You've got such a spring in your step, it's as though your little legs were made of air.

LEON:
I'll get that ball of hair. Why, it looks like a rat. I'll have to use a smaller bat. I'll wait till Jen's not looking then I'll do the ghastly beast in.

JEN VALJEAN:
I sure did miss my dog friends even though I now have some human companions. Aha, here we are at the Bodega. Let's see what can I get ya? How about a little bone, and for Larrondo, I'll get some smokes. I'll just tie your leash to this little tree. Now, be good and wait for me!

Ah, what a great day. I've a little pay from walking dogs today. The sun is shining. It's a balmy March day. Hallo, sir, I'll take some cigs, and this bone, no bigger than a twig. For Uristat, I'll take a Snickers. Thanks Mister!

La, la, la… Oh Jen Valjean Junior, I have returned…

Aaaaaaaaaaaaaaaaaah! What is this that I see? Little Jen Valjean Junior stretched out in front of me! From its hind legs it doth bleed. Its tiny mouth is open in a whimper and a cry. Why, Lord oh why have you forsaken me, and who hath bludgeoned this tiny beast, and what is this? Someone dropped their keys at the crime scene, and wouldn't you know it bears a Mercedes logo! The evil that dwells in the heart of these landlords is more than this world can afford. I shall avenge this brutal attack. I will pay him back, but first, Jen Junior needs an animal doctor. I know there is a vet on Tenth Street. I better move my feet. Here frail hound. I shall scoop you up in a tiny mound and carry your limp body through the streets, and then, when you are cared for, I shall visit Misrahi! Please don't cry sweet little fawn-dog. It won't be long.

Ah, finally, I have arrived. My quivering thighs broke all Olympic records to get you here on time. Hallo, I have an animal emergency. I need your help please!

VET RECEPTIONIST:
Do you have insurance?

JEN VALJEAN:
No, but I have some change in the pockets of my pants.

VET RECEPTIONIST:
Sorry, we don't see unemployed losers. We're a legit business here.

JEN VALJEAN:
But, I have a job! I'm a dog walker!

VET RECEPTIONIST:
Then, whose fault is it dear?

JEN VALJEAN:
But, I only stopped to get it a bone.

VET RECEPTIONIST:
Moan, moan, moan; that's all you people ever do. Maybe if you didn't complain, there'd be some benefits for you. I can't help it if you don't have insurance. Do I look like Miss Moneybags?

JEN VALJEAN:
But, it's a dog, for CHRISSAKES!

VET RECEPTIONIST:
And, I am not to blame for the policy. Hello, security, we've got a crazy woman in the lobby.

JEN VALJEAN:
You! You stinking rats! You won't even help a dying dog!

SECURITY:
Cuckoo house is where she belongs. Come on, you're goin'. Take your little sidekick with you.

JEN VALJEAN:
Could it be true? Yes, it is! The world really is a pile of shit. Jen Valjean Junior dies in my arms. I can take it no longer!

DREAMY VISION OF CHORUS OF RATS:
You must be stronger! You must be stronger!

JEN VALJEAN:
The rats, they come to me in a dream like vision. I find solace in their infinite wisdom.

DREAMY VISION OF CHORUS OF RATS:
There is a nurse named Big Mike Hogan. He works the nightshift at Presbyterian. He is a good man and will help you for free. Go to his placc on 5th and B, buzzer 3C.

JEN VALJEAN:
Vision; don't fail me now, each growing minute is another blow to the fragile form, which cries in my arms. How could anyone harm such a gentle beast?

Here we are, 5th and B.

BIG MIKE:
Hallo, who is it?

JEN VALJEAN:
My name is Jen. I need your help. Let me in.

BIG MIKE:
You sound desperate. Come right up.

Holy Fuck! Who did this?

JEN VALJEAN:
A total dick who goes by the name of Leon Misrahi.

BIG MIKE:
I know the name well. It's one of infamy. Well, we better get to work. First things first, painkillers to stop the hurt.

(Insert psychedelic music, such as "White Rabbit" to insinuate Jen Valjean Junior is about to be psychedelicized.)

JEN VALJEAN JUNIOR:
All right! Dig it! Let's get it on! Come on Doctor man, don't be so stingy, I got me some broken bones. Groooooooveeeee!

BIG MIKE:
OK, it appears the painkillers have set in. Now the surgery can begin.

JEN VALJEAN JUNIOR:
Yo, Florence Nightingale, don't blow my cool! I ain't no fool! More drugs, more drugs, more drugs.

BIG MIKE:
I tell ya what I'd do to these thugs! To hurt an innocent animal—the worst kinda criminal.

JEN VALJEAN:
Thank you so much for helping. The other place wasn't so friendly. You work so quickly and so efficiently.

BIG MIKE:
Yeah, I used to work in the animal ER, until I got busted for stealing special K, and dealing it in bars. Now I help animals as a public service.

JEN VALJEAN:
What kind of device is this?

BIG MIKE:
It's a tiny wheelchair. I've already set the fractures. These little casts will have to last for a month. This here is an Elizabethan collar to keep the critter from biting the stitches out.

JEN VALJEAN JUNIOR:
Look out! I look like a damn freak! Oh man, the room is spinning and I am getting sleepy. Yeah, nice and slow that is the tempo, slow and low…Oh look, a bunny!

JEN VALJEAN:
She looks so peaceful.

BIG MIKE:
It's really remarkable.

JEN VALJEAN:
I don't have much money, but I would certainly like to pay you.

BIG MIKE:
Nah, I don't need money. What I want you to do is drive that bastard out of this city. For him, I have no pity.

JEN VALJEAN:
Thank you, Big Mike.

BIG MIKE:
No problem.

JEN VALJEAN JUNIOR:
Yeah, thanks for making me look like a total fucking dork.

Scene Fourteen

URISTAT:
My elvin-love, you are home. All night, I have roamed the city, looking for thee.

JEN VALJEAN:
My story, it is rather frightening. The beloved Chihuahua whom I walk each morn. Its legs were broken and torn by none other than our beloved landlord.

URISTAT:
Good lord. This means war!

JEN VALJEAN:
The good news is I picked us up a new Mercedes, courtesy of

Misrahi. Care to go for a ride?

URISTAT:
I shall abide!

JEN VALJEAN:
To Misrahi's office on Rivington Street, where the Xeroxes are always free! It's two in the morning and I've got a key!

URISTAT:
Yippeeee!

JEN VALJEAN:
Yeah, his car it rides like a dream, and I found these pictures under the seat!

URISTAT:
Oh no! They are of Misrahi, wearing a diaper. He's sucking on a pacifier. This just isn't right here. Is that his wife?

JEN VALJEAN:
If his wife has a penis.

URISTAT:
Oh shit! I didn't see that one. Wow! She's well-hung. That's a big whip in her hand. What's that being rammed…forget it.

JEN VALJEAN:
I don't know, but the end is lit.

URISTAT:
It's bigger than a baby's arm.

JEN VALJEAN:
It is bigger than a barn! Such Kodak moments bring tears to my eyes.

URISTAT:
He's such a tough guy. I just can't believe.

JEN VALJEAN:
Neither will his wife, Mimi.

URISTAT:
I see, I see. You are a masterful thief.

JEN VALJEAN:
My time in prison taught me a great many things, but mostly a hatred for hypocrisy. For instance, Mayor McSleaze, he likes to get

down on his knees and pretend to be a puppy. I know from a cellmate who he paid a great deal of money to train him on newspaper. It really is a shame that people aren't more honest here.

URISTAT:
Looking at these, I almost pity him.

JEN VALJEAN:
Me too, but then I think on little Jen Valjean, my dog-friend, who might never walk again.

URISTAT:
You are right. He is a bastard and we should plaster these allover the town!

JEN VALJEAN:
Here we are don't make a sound, till we're inside. Here, take this flashlight. The copier is on the left. We must be quick. We must be deft.

URISTAT:
I will enlarge these to 300 percent.

JEN VALJEAN:
That should make a dent in their ink supply. In the meanwhile, I will open up their files. Oh look, their accounting books. I think I'll have a look. Oh look, they're charging $1,700 for a studio. What a crook! These books have gotta go! First I slice them in the paper cutter. Then I'll hit the paper shredder. When Leon arrives tomorrow, he will have to borrow a pot to piss in.

URISTAT:
What fun this is!

JEN VALJEAN:
I am jotting down the cost of each tenant's rent and tomorrow I will pay them back, but first I have to find out where the money's at!

URISTAT:
We'll have to ransack this place. Oh look—a safe!

JEN VALJEAN:
Hand it to me. I've got a hunch what the numbers might be—666. Look, it did the trick!

URISTAT:
Wow, these wads of cash are thick!

JEN VALJEAN:
Here—Let's fill the backpack and get back to our slum. There, we'll count the sum, and in the morning, we'll deliver the cash to our neighbors. It will be a holiday on the LES. People will party. It will be the best.

URISTAT:
I have never seen so much money in all my years. Hey, do you wanna stop for beers?

JEN VALJEAN:
No we should get home. I'm sure the cops are starting to roam looking for the hot Mercedes. I don't wanna act crazy.

URISTAT:
You are right, let's go.

JEN VALJEAN:
Wait a second—what is that light? It is so bright. It blinds me.

URISTAT:
The sirens are alarming!

COP #1:
Hold it right there, Jen Valjean!

JEN VALJEAN:
They don't see you. Hide until I go. Take the money. You know what to do.

URISTAT:
I do, and I will come for you. We will tear down the walls. Don't lose hope.

JEN VALJEAN:
Go! Just go!

COP #2:
What's wrong, Jen? Couldn't stay away? You missed the inmates? Not having any luck at Meow Mix?

JEN VALJEAN:
Screw you filthy swine. There'll come a time when the tables are turned and you're the ones who are forced to learn what it's like to take a rusty dildo up the ass!

COP #1:
Enough of your sass, get in the car. We always knew you were a

career criminal not good enough to clean a urinal. Come on, Jen, why don't you beg for mercy. You know I find elf juice rather tasty.

JEN VALJEAN:
I don't have to beg because in a few days, I'll be free.

COP #2:
Who's gonna save you; that miserable queen? Stop dreaming! Your beloved Queeny is snorting lines off Keanu's ass. Guess the revolution didn't last. It's funny how quick he went from being a starving tenant to a gay socialite, tramp.

JEN VALJEAN:
Don't talk shit about Larrondo. He's good people, I should know. You only talk this shit cause you're all in the closet. You're all a bunch of angry queens who can't handle it!

COP #1:
Another word outta you and we'll see it to it that solitary's available—always makes a nice stable for an elf.

JEN VALJEAN:
You'll see for yourself just how wrong you are. I won't stay behind bars.

COP #2:
Are a little group of mice gonna steal a key and make you free, just like in Cinderella! Maybe they'll even sew you a dress. Maybe they'll find you a fella!

COP #1:
Ha! She doesn't want no fella. Hey—Jen, you gonna bust outta prison in a giant pumpkin?

JEN VALJEAN:
Fuck you, scum.

COP #2:
Too bad your fairy Godmother's at Twilo with a dick down his throat!

JEN VALJEAN:
Twilo's not even open any more! Mayor McSleaze closed its doors. But you squares aren't even aware of that! You're too busy taking it up the ass in your very own station house.

COP #1:
Listen you louse. One more word outta you, and you'll get a fresh new bruise.

COP #2:
Here we are! I am sure your former inmates are wet with anticipation to greet New York's newest star.

COP #1:
Lookee who we got here ladies!

BURLY FEMALE PRISONER #1:
Mmm, elf meat!

BURLY FEMALE PRISONER #2:
Yahhooooeeee! Ya been gone too long, girlee. You sure look pretty.

JEN VALJEAN:
Leave me alone, all of you!

BURLY FEMALE PRISONER #1:
Boohoohoo, got used to the free life, eh Jen? Don't ever depend on it.

BURLY FEMALE PRISONER #2:
You're a lifer you can bet.

BURLY FEMALE PRISONER #1:
Hey, Jen, they're shooting a new episode of Scared Straight tomorrow. Wanna play my nasty ho? You can tell the people what it's like to lick my vulva every night!

JEN VALJEAN:
I will have no part of your vulva this night or any. In less than a week, I'll be free.

BURLY FEMALE PRISONER #2:
Awe, that's so cute, you still have hope. Give it up you silly dope! Wait…let me guess, you met a dude, whose heart you wooed and he promised to help you get free. I know, it happened to me. You wait one week, then two, not a letter, not a clue. On visiting days you stare through the glass, and when no one's there, you feel like an ass. Guess what Jen? He's not coming. Chances are there's a new girl he's screwing.

BURLY FEMALE PRISONER #1:
Yeah, Jen give up. All guys suck.

JEN VALJEAN:
I know I sound naïve but I still believe that he will come.

BURLY FEMALE PRISONER #2:
Yeah, he'll come…on his new girlfriend! Ha! You think you know

men? You've got a lot to learn about that sex, most importantly they're all dastardly. They're cheating, stealing lying cretins who should only be used for breeding. Forget about them. You're here for good. Don't make it worse by crying about some dude.

JEN VALJEAN *(to self)*:
But, he wasn't just a dude. He was kind. He was good. Oh, Uristat, I know where your heart's at. It beats with mine as I lie in this cage filled with insurmountable rage. I know you will come for me, but then again, why do I believe? Most humans are cruel and deceitful. How can my heart be so trustful? In a couple days we shall see if I am too filled with naiveté.

Scene Fifteen

LARRONDO:
Jesus Christ, what is that banging? It's eight in the morning, and I've only had an hour's rest. I want to look my best tomorrow for *Vanity Fair*! Who the hell is there?

URISTAT:
Larrondo, it's me, Uristat, you've got to let me in! Something terrible has happened!

LARRONDO:
Let me guess—you broke Jen's hymen—oh wait—that was a week ago. I know! I was forced to watch while coated in ice.

URISTAT:
Larrondo, there has been strife! Jen Valjean is in prison again. She's under lock and key.

LARRONDO:
What do you need—bail money?

URISTAT:
This is a no-bail situation. We've got to bust her out of prison.

LARRONDO:
Are you nuts? This isn't escape from Alcatraz. Listen, I'm turning into a tired old hag, and I've got a photo shoot tomorrow.

URISTAT:
You can't go!

LARRONDO:
What do you mean? It's *Vanity Fair*—you know the magazine?

URISTAT;
If only you had seen the tears in her eyes, when they carted her away. I'm afraid she's there to stay. They were so cruel, with their homophobic insults and their pointing out her every fault.

LARRONDO:
Did you say homophobic?

URISTAT:
Indeed, the reprobates!

LARRONDO:
Damn, I hate those angry queens. I guess I've seen enough of the limelight. It's time to fight and keep it real.

URISTAT:
That's what I like to hear! The good news is, when we were busted, we were raiding Misrahi's cabinet, and I've got a wad of cash to sink a ship. We can pay our army with it!

LARRONDO:
What say we do?

URISTAT:
Barrel through the walls of the Women's penitentiary. Set her free.

LARRONDO:
We can't just barrel in. It's a high security prison. We need a plan…

CHORUS OF RATS:
Can we lend a hand?

LARRONDO:
Again, it's the rats in togas. I know I've done plenty of acid in my day, but what is going on?

CHORUS OF RATS:
We are Jen's advisors. All along, we have guided her. This trouble she is in is no mistake. Everything is in its place for an elvin revolution. Our solution is simple. We are small and we are nimble. We can waltz right into the prison unnoticed; there we will inject the guards with a substance known as morphine. When the guards fall fast asleep, we'll steal a key! Voila! She is free! But this is not enough. If we free her from prison without doing anything more she will

always be running from the law, and so we must free all the non-violent offenders—the petty thieves, the pot smokers. We must burn the rent-books, evict the landlords, and take our city back.

LARRONDO:
What do you want with a hack like me?

CHORUS OF RATS:
Your new found infamy. It will help our cause.

LARRONDO:
Whatever you say boss. Keanu can wait till after the revolution to taste my sweet, sweet lovin'. Where do we start?

URISTAT:
We each have a part. Larrondo, you and I must round up all the underdogs.

CHORUS OF RATS:
That's right, anyone who's done no wrong but who's felt the iron fist of this piece of shit city government—you know the squeegee guys, the pretzel vendors, the topless dancers, the hookers, the squatters, the cabbies, the teachers, the students with no books to read.

LARRONDO:
The list is massive indeed. And, don't forget about the Mets or the gays who can't wed, or the homeless without a bed, or the millions with no health insurance and the tenants paying too much rent!

CHORUS OF RATS:
We'll all gather outside of the prison! It will be great fun! When Jen is released we will head back to Misrahi's. The time of exorbitant rents shall be no more! Decent housing for the poor!

LARRONDO:
There's just one thing that's bothering me. No one mentioned that this was Marxist puppetry—that is so '99.

URISTAT:
Quit your bitching we have no time. Reverend Jen only made this a puppet show because she's sick of actors. Puppets are nice and show up for rehearsal.

CHORUS OF RATS:
Yeah, and who said Marxist puppetry is over? It never reached it's full potential. Reverend Jen's just improving it by adding a puppet sex scene it will be a bigger hit than any puppet show in history.

LARRONDO:
Whatever! A 60-page puppet show? The bitch is crazy. Plus, she's drunk all the time.

URISTAT:
Don't blame her!

LARRONDO:
She tries to move us while holding a Budweiser!

URISTAT:
If it weren't for her, none of us would exist. So, her puppetry skills aren't the best.

LARRONDO:
Her puppet theater is an old refrigerator box with a hole cut in it and her cardboard puppets look like shit. She is an embarrassment to the entire world of puppetry. I am embarrassed to be in this play. Why can't she take Misrahi to landlord tenant court like a normal person?

URISTAT:
She hasn't the time, and this is more fun!

LARRONDO:
Oh, but she has time to write forced rhymes all day long. To which parallel universe does she belong?

CHORUS OF RATS:
OK, Larrondo, I think you've broken the fourth wall. Now, can we please get back to the show?

LARRONDO:
Sure. I'll pretend like this never happened. I'm so happy to be in puppet land! La, la, la, la… So, as you were saying, we'll be paying Jen a visit, with the various misfits whom we can get.

CHORUS OF RATS:
Exactly, in one week's time, Mayor McSleeze will realize that the citizens are no longer appeased by talk alone. When he goes to his office, he'll find that it's gone.

URISTAT:
And, who on earth will run the city? I don't have enough faith in humans to believe in anarchy.

CHORUS OF RATS:
You are perceptive Uristat. Anarchy would be realistic if humans weren't such dicks. We'll leave anarchy to be embraced by the punk

rock youths who hang out on Saint Mark's Place. We rats have plans to take up office once we oust that offensive puppet. The Mayoral seat will be filled with rats and only one human representative. Everything will be decided by a vote of the residents. No more bought elections! No more corporate contributions! Ours shall be a city run for the rats, the people, and the stray dogs and cats by the people and the rats!

LARRONDO:
And what of the mayor's residence, Lacey Mansion?

CHORUS OF RATS:
It will become a center for elf-eared orphans!

LARRONDO:
And will you fix the subways?

CHORUS OF RATS:
Not only will we fix the public transportation, we'll put a live teletubby in every station and a kaleidoscopic light show in every car. Every 6 seats will feature a bar! The trains'll run on time and they'll only cost a dime. The subway buskers will have jobs on each car entertaining wide and far.

URISTAT:
It sounds too expensive! Surely you smoke crack!

CHORUS OF RATS:
Actually, the subways will be such a hit; it'll be tough to get a ticket! People will dump their cars in lieu of the hot new subway bars. We'll be able to build more lines. We'll build a subway up to Mars! And, that's not all, subway stations will have clean bathroom stalls, and we'll build self-cleaning public toilets throughout the city. It will be a new era for small bladder citizenry.

LARRONDO:
It sounds rather noisy, rather cramped.

CHORUS OF RATS:
We'll build meditation stations to deal with that—glowing rooms where people can sit in peace and quiet, or suck on Oxygen if they wish. People will benefit from it—not so many people will get sick—of course we'll socialize healthcare, and we'll legalize drugs to pay for it! Also, Richard Simmons will hold an office in which he encourages citizens to stay fit.

URISTAT:
Sounds like you rats have it all figured out, but it won't be fair to

steal an election. What makes you think the people will vote you in?

CHORUS OF RATS:
When they hear our plan, they will be amazed. It will be a bright new day! We'll legalize nudity and we'll legalize drugs. We'll make sure orphans get lots of hugs. Hospitals won't treat the poor like shit, and the elderly will have a place to sit as they wait for the bus. In us rats the people will trust for we are wise despite ours size, we will run the city efficiently.

LARRONDO:
I am starting to see. Let's get moving. It's about time we had some public nudity. It's time the people began to sing!

CHORUS OF RATS:
Can you hear the vermin sing?

LARRONDO:
Can you hear the gay men sing?

URISTAT:
Can you hear the homeless sing?

CHORUS OF RATS:
Will you join in our crusade?

SQUEEGEE GUYS:
Can you hear the squeegee men sing?

TOPLESS DANCERS:
Can you hear the strippers sing?

PRETZEL GUYS:
Can you hear the pretzel vendors sing?

THE METS:
Can you hear the Mets sing?

CHORUS OF RATS:
Do you hear the people's song? They will not be slaves again.

LARRONDO:
Unless that's what they're into.

ALL:
Can you hear the people sing? Can you hear us Misrahi? We will not pay any more fees to live on your squalid property!

LARRONDO:
With no hot water and no heat!

CHORUS OF RATS:
And a leak in the ceiling!

THE METS:
While the roaches live for free!

PRETZEL GUYS:
And the plaster crumbles freely!

ALL:
We are headed to the prison! We are on a mission! We will sing an avant-garde musical puppet show until you let us know that you've given up!

Scene Sixteen

JEN VALJEAN *(to be sung softly)*:
Oh where oh where is my Uristat? It's been four days. Where could he be at? I was a fool to be duped by love. Call me Ophelia for like Hamlet, he gained my trust, and now I look for a way to end my life. Is there something to tie around my neck? I shall hang myself rather than continue to live with the horrid smell of this prison…

FEMALE PRISONER #1:
Hey Cinderella, where's your carriage? Did it turn into a pumpkin already?

FEMALE PRISONER #2:
Yeah, I think your prince found someone new to bang! I heard he had a three way with the ugly stepsisters!

FEMALE PRISONER #1:
Ah, good one! Hey Jen, I think you need to run to Duane Reade cause that was a total burn.

JEN VALJEAN:
That is the last time you will ever spurn this young elf. I have decided to kill myself.

FEMALE PRISONER #2:
Well, if you need any help let us know. I am sick of hearing you moan. Say, do you have any cigs, I'm all out?

ODIUS:
What's wrong? Is the little elf continuing to pout? Boo-fuckin-hoo. I'll tell you what to do! Get back to work you lazy cunt if not, I'll kill you myself ya little runt. We've got fifty thousand license plates to make by Thursday. Do you hear what I say? Don't just stand there like you're deaf, or do you still think someone's gonna save your neck?

FEMALE PRISONER #1:
Yeah, she's still waitin' on the little mice to make her a pretty new dress and unlock her cell!

CHORUS OF RATS (*sneaking up behind*):
Here we are. It smells like hell. The big one in gray must be the guard. She looks dumb. This shouldn't be too hard. We will wait till she turns the corner. That's when we'll jab her with the needle.

ODIUS:
All right you stinking piles of dog shit. I'm going outside for a bit.

(*Move puppet off-stage*)

ODIUS (O.S.):
What the hell? Ah, I am beginning to smell the scent of flowers. What cute mice. Oh look a bunny rabbit! I am so gay and so happy…

FEMALE PRISONER #2:
Hey Jen, you heard what Odius said! Get to work knucklehead!

FEMALE PRISONER #1:
Oh come on—Odius is gone. That would be a waste of fun! I've got a better idea on how we can put this elf to work! Come here, little girl!

(*Female prisoners grope Jen.*)

JEN VALJEAN:
Back off you hideous Beasts!

FEMALE PRISONER #2:
Oh, come on we're just havin' an elf meat feast. Better get used to it now that you're hear for eternity.

JEN VALJEAN:
Get your slimy hands off of me!

FEMALE PRISONER #2:
But, look Jen; I've got a shiny new metal dildo!

FEMALE PRISONER #1:
And wouldn't you know, I've got a barbwire butt plug to go with it!

JEN VALJEAN:
Please no! I'm going to be sick!

FEMALE PRISONER #1:
Oh come on Jen, might as well face it. Your fairy godmother's not gonna save ya!

Larrondo arrives, carrying a weapon.

LARRONDO:
Think again you fiendish ghouls! Better go back to etiquette school. Raping fellow inmates with homemade dildos is simply not proper. This stun gun ought to stop ya!

He fires. They fall!

LARRONDO:
Come on Jen, we're goin' home.

ODIUS:
Not so fast you talking gnome. I've awoken from my drug-induced coma. Nice trick, but now I've got ya! And, I'll fight you bare-fisted if that's what it takes. Jen's not getting by these gates. She's stayin' here till her pubes turn gray, and I'm gonna personally check 'em every day. How do ya like that you intrusive faggot?

LARRONDO:
You slimy maggot; I'll step on you till you ooze goo!

ODIUS:
Not if I sit on you; you fucking fruit!

Odius sits on Larrondo.

LARRONDO:
No! No! I'm being crushed alive!

Uristat appears.

URISTAT:
Jen! I'm so happy you're alive!

JEN VALJEAN:
Uristat! Let me look into your eyes.

The two kiss passionately.

LARRONDO:
OK. This isn't a fucking Big Red commercial. This is all really special, but would you mind getting this 400-pound dyke off of me?

JEN VALJEAN:
Certainly. Uristat; is it a fact that you know karate?

URISTAT:
Not really, but I was once rented Curtis Sleewa's self defense video from Kim's on Ave. A .

ODIUS:
Ha, ha, ha, ha… Die you spindly gay loser.

URISTAT:
But, luckily the rats gave me some weapons to use here. I wonder what this one does?

JEN VALJEAN:
Oh no! You just blew the guard's head off.

URISTAT:
Oops. Well, I guess we can go. Larrondo, are you OK?

LARRONDO:
I'm traumatized for life and I think she crushed my spine, but I can move enough to leave this hellhole.

JEN VALJEAN:
Then to freedom we shall go.

URISTAT:
The people, Jen; they wait outside for you, carrying torches and their ripped up leases. On Misrahi Realty many have already descended.

JEN VALJEAN:
Then to Rivington Street we must go!

URISTAT:
The rats have procured us a pedi-cab, which will take us there in half the time! Do you hear the singing? Do you see the signs?

JEN VALJEAN (*singing*):
Yes. I hear the people sing! They sing a song of angry tenants! They sing a song of lower rents! They sing a song that says we're through with overpriced squalid studios!

URISTAT:
Yes! I hear the people sing! They sing of legalized dance and open containers! They sing of a world that's markedly saner.

ALL:
Yes, we hear the people sing, singing angry chants throughout the city! Can you hear us Mr. Misrahi? Can you hear us Mayor McSleaze!

Scene Seventeen

MISRAHI:
Ah! Nothing like sitting in my private office on a Monday afternoon having nothing to do but download porn while my flunkies take the scorn of tenants throughout the LES. To be the boss is the best! Thank God I've got my own water cooler so I don't have to run into the fools that work here. Things have been so calm and reserved since that elf-bitch got what she deserved. In fact, they've been a little too quiet. The phones haven't rung. There hasn't been a riot! Fix my ceiling! The toilet's leaking! A rat ate my cat! SHUT UP! Give it a rest. Ooh! Analinvaders.com! That's going on the favorites page no prob!

The sound of a phone ringing.

MISRAHI (*cont'd*):
Hello!

MIMI:
You bastard!

MISRAHI:
So nice to hear from you; to what do I owe the pleasure?

MIMI:
Haven't seen the paper today yet, have you? Bad enough you have a mistress, but—Leon; a dude? I am leaving you and I am taking the house, the kids and every goddamn thing you own!

MISRAHI:
No! Mimi. Don't!

MIMI:
You're gonna have to live in a nasty flea-covered walk-up like all the rest of the scum!

She hangs up.

MISRAHI:
Never did I think Mimi would leave. It seems my gifts always appeased her desires, and now, to think—when I retire, I will grow old and die alone and perhaps without a home. I wonder if this day could get worse.

SECRETARY:
Mr. Misrahi! You must come at once! The sidewalk's so full it's going to burst! There is mayhem outside.

MISRAHI:
Shit. Don't tell anyone I'm here. I'm going to hide.

SECRETARY:
I am sorry sir. I cannot do that. For years, we have taken the crap that should've been handed to you. Because it's my job I was always willing to do what you told me to do, but I will not stand out there and be made an idiot because you are not man enough to handle this shit. I quit! In fact, I'm joining the protesters. Make your own fucking coffee you balding piece of sleaze.

MISRAHI:
Don't go! I don't know how to make coffee! Please somebody help me!

PROTESTERS:
Can you hear the people sing? Can you hear us Misrahi? We will not pay your exorbitant rents! We would rather live in tents!

JEN VALJEAN:
You thought you could cheat us forever, Misrahi? You thought if you turned off the heat, we wouldn't bother to get out of bed. You thought if you kept us down, we'd lay down for dead; that if you turned off the water, we'd stay inside cause we felt dirty. Let me tell you—this is our city! It is not a city of rich land-owning tyrants, but a place for urchins and artists! A place for dreamers who breathe life into this place, where its OK to not have as much space or a four-car garage or a barrage of bedrooms and a well-trimmed lawn, but it's more important to stay up till dawn, creating, dancing, laughing and living. This is what you're missing and in doing so you

are killing the city. Making it unaffordable for the most incredible people—the poor who know how to party. Now I hand the megaphone to those holding the mayoral seat.

CHORUS OF RATS:
Misrahi! Come out of your office or we will come and get you! We are the new city government! The Lower East Side is now its own republic and Mayor McSleaze has been sent to Governor's Island, which has been converted into a giant amusement park for poor children. He is working the giant swings. Your job will be to rip tickets outside of the haunted house. The chief of police is working the ferris wheel. The parks commissioner is working the bumper cars, spreading joy near and far. You can smoke all the weed you want there or you can dance at the all night bar, but you must never ever attempt to gain or misuse power again. You shall never lord over land again. Plus, you must pay one million dollars to the animal shelter as reparations for your disregard for the health of poor chihuahua Jen Valjean Junior.

MISRAHI:
You can't do this! You're not even human!

CHORUS OF RATS:
Ah yes, but we are your oldest tenants.

MISRAHI:
This is my worst fear!

CHORUS OF RATS:
Don't fret my dear. Far from being vindictive we believe in rehabilitation, and for a model we looked to your primate cousin, the Bonobo chimpanzee, a fascinating species, which values sex over power—any squabbles over food are quickly diluted when the Bonobos rub up against each other in a rather heated manner, and that is why we are also sending your she-male partner to "Jen Valjean's Amusement Park for the Poor." The two of you can bury your heads in each others noggins till the stars fall from the sky—soon you will forget all about your former life. Power won't seem so important when weighed against some good clean lovin'.

MISRAHI:
What about Mimi?

CHORUS OF RATS:
Well, she'll get what she always wanted—half of everything!

MISRAHI:
This sounds like a Hollywood ending!

JEN VALJEAN:
Not until Uristat kisses me!

LARRONDO:
I've seen enough! Plus, I'm sure Jen's puppeteers are probably too drunk to hold us at this point so for the sake of the audience can

we just get on with it? Jesus! Let's just sing already!

ALL:
> Sing of a city that is fun.
>
> Where dancing is legal and so is nudity.
>
> Where the land is not governed by stupidity!
>
> Where gay marriage is legal and so is weed!
>
> Where the children in school have books to read!
>
> That's the kind of city we want!
>
> Sing of a city that is affordable. Sing of leaders that are dependable.
>
> Where Mayors don't buy elections and landlords don't rob their tenants!
>
> Sing a song of a bright new day where the voiceless and tired will be happy and gay!
>
> (At this point, two midgets wielding trumpets should appear at either side of the puppet theater, and blow their trumpets.)
>
> Listen to the people sing!
>
> Listen to the rats sing!
>
> They sing a song of joy today for the overthrow of Misrahi.
>
> They sing a song of happy elves!
>
> Where people are free of 9 to 5 hell!
>
> That's the kind of city we need.
>
> Where the people are joyful, the people are free...

MAKE YOUR OWN Puppets!
CUT ALONG THE DOTTED LINE,
TAPE TO A STICK AND YOUR SET!
THEN DRAW YOUR OWN! NEAT!
JEN VAIJEAN
CHORUS OF RATS
JEN VAIJEAN JUNIOR

About Reverend Jen Junior

Reverend Jen Junior is a champagne-blonde chihuahua. Even though she is descended from wolves, she weighs only four pounds. Because chihuahuas come from Mexico, they almost never win at the dog shows, which are racist. The next time you watch a dog show, note that the chihuahuas are always the cutest, but the other dogs always win. Reverend Jen Junior's hobbies are tearing up tissue, playing with her monkey stuffed animal, going to the small dog / dog run, chasing cats and stealthily sneaking trolls out of the troll museum. She dislikes people with "bad vibes," the smell of nail polish, and being called "rat dog." (Look for her autobiography, "Don't Call Me Rat Dog.") Currently, she is at work on her own line of chihuahua clothing – "International Girl."

If you look closely at Reverend Jen Junior, you'll notice that she is actually an elf trapped in the body of a dog.

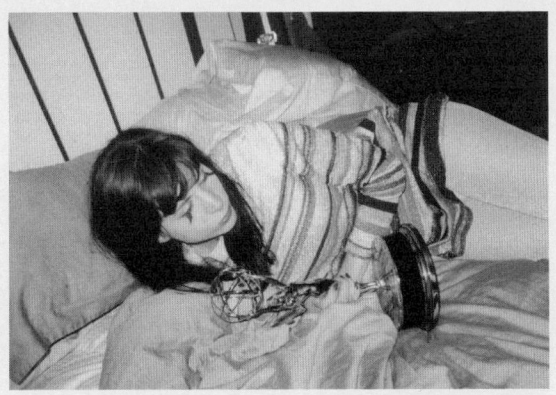

Photo: Shaolin

About the Author

Saint Reverend Jen is one of the busiest humans who ever roamed the earth. She is a poet, preacher, painter, prophet, upcoming celebrity/personality, Troll Museum founder and curator, amateur wrestler, underground movie star, unsuccessful capitalist, beer enthusiast, Voice of the Downtrodden and Tired and Patron Saint of the Uncool. She is the author of several self-published books including *Beer is Magic* and *Sex Symbol for the Insane*. Her essay on ear-wax removal addiction was recently published in *Aroused*, a collection of erotic writing (edited by Karen Finley) and her rant on sea monkeys was recently published in *101 Damnations, The Humorists' Tour of Personal Hells* (from Saint Martin's Press). She used to be a columnist for *SHOUT* until she got canned for not being cool enough. As usual, she turned the lemon into lemonade and started her own magazine, *ASS* (Art Star Scene Magazine.) Currently, she is at work on her most ambitious project to date, Rev. Jen Worldwide, a corporation whose goal is to promote non-boring existence through art.

Today, Saint Reverend Jen lives in her Troll Museum on the Lower East Side with Saint Reverend Jen Junior, a Chihuahua.

End?

The

"I don't know. He's a professional model," Matt said.

"What? Now even the squatters are more successful than me. This sucks." I said.

I then began to inquire a bit more about the squat. According to a youth who was carrying a giant bottle of Mountain Dew, the squat is now actually owned by the government. The government rents the squat! I couldn't friggin' believe it. Even the squats have landlords. I hope and pray that this is not the future of New York, but unfortunately, everywhere you look there's a goddamn landlord taking money from someone who is working so hard to pay the douchebag that they've forgotten how to live, and all the artists, are becoming like Travis Bickle—angry and tired of the bullshit. But, where do we go? The answer is, there's nowhere else to go, and if there is, I sure as Hell don't know where it is. I guess that's the future.

I know I'll stay here for as long as I can until another screwball incompetent doctor misdiagnoses a ruptured organ as gas and I die or until I become so hugely famous that I am forced to move to a sequestered home in a neighborhood the whereabouts of which I cannot reveal for fear of being stalked and harassed, where I will sit by my pool with Reverend Jen Junior fondly reminiscing about the magical world we once inhabited.

Chapter Sixteen
What the Future Holds

Last weekend my friend, Eden, invited me to a party at a squat. I didn't know that any squats still existed so I went just to see for myself. As my friend, Tom, and I wandered up Avenue C, he said, "This is where I used to get my heroin." But as we looked around we saw nothing but bistros, cafes and bars. Occasionally we'd see one so hip looking that we'd stop in our tracks and exclaim, "Holy shit! Look at that one!" like Andy and Ducky pointing out mansions in *Pretty in Pink*. When we got to 9th Street, I realized I had forgotten the exact address of said squat, but then I saw two young, mohawked kids sitting on a stoop who seemed to be absorbed in angst. I approached them in my bright pink overcoat. "Excuse me," I asked, "Is there a squat around here?"

"Yeah, but you might not wanna go in there. There's a mosh pit," they said.

I told them I thought I could handle it, and they escorted Tom and me into the building. Inside there were several adorable "squatters." I knew that I wanted to have disenfranchised kids pose for the cover of my book and I thought this might be a goldmine of cover models. I saw my friend, Matt, an NYU student who "borrowed" lights for *Lord of the Cockrings*. "These are your friends, right?" I asked him.

"Yeah."

"Do you think they would pose for my book?" I asked.

"Yeah."

Just then, I saw a boy in a tattered leather jacket with four-foot-high spikes in his hair. He looked like he hadn't eaten in a week. "He's perfect!" I exclaimed.

Photo: Maurice Narcis

place is also nameless, but has already been deemed a necessity by locals who remember the days when we lost change in the vending machines whilst doing our laundry. Now there's this handy place in which to get sprinkled donuts and coffee while tackling that most annoying of chores.

Upon writing this chapter, I realize that I almost never go out to eat, but I also never cook so I'm trying to figure out how it is that I remain alive. I eat a lot of power bars even though they taste like ass. There are a few other places, which are probably good, but now I'm thinking you should just look on citysearch.com because I'm really tired of writing about food. In fact, I am tired of writing. I am hungry. I have to pee and Reverend Jen Junior is trying to eat my laptop. I think it's time for a conclusion and then a puppet show!

Three varieties of pickles!

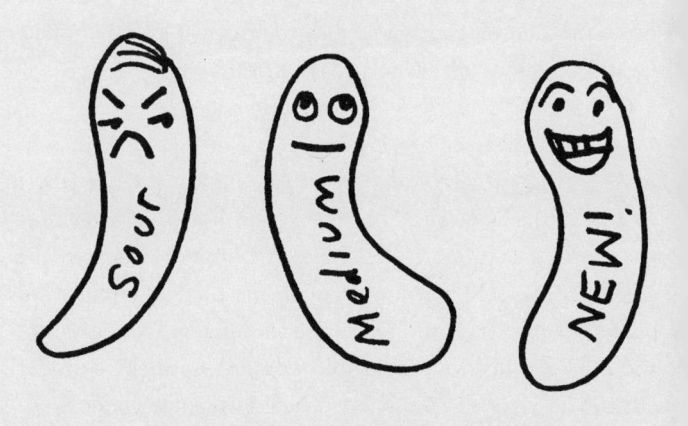

Sour Medium NEW!

Saint "Lucifer's" as I refer to it) and I was forced to go without food for seven days, several friends offered to "fatten" me back up by taking me out for free meals. Had my appendix never ruptured, I probably would have never eaten at this fine French establishment, but alas, the lemon was turned into lemonade, and I must say the food here is quite sumptuous. I had some cod thing that was completely soaked in butter. In fact everything there is soaked in butter so much so that the whole place smells like butter. The bread was soft and hot and the wine was fantastic. Now if I could only get another organ to give out, I might get a second meal there.

Earth Matters (177 Ludlow St.): This organic food store opened only a short time ago, but it has already become popular with LES residents who were looking for a healthier source of food than the axis of fat at the food court. Here you can get soy hot dogs, organic coffee and a whole array of fake meat products as well as many other healthy treats.

Grilled Cheese (168 Ludlow St.): I have only been here once, and admittedly, going there made me feel like the laziest wastrel in the Western Hemisphere. Am I so lazy that I can't just make a frigging grilled cheese at home? However, the grilled cheeses sold here are much fancier than anything you'd probably make at home. They have all different types of bread and toppings that your probably wouldn't normally consider putting on a grilled cheese, but which taste quite good.

Rush Hour (Ludlow right above Rivington): This little store seems to have already gone through several name changes, but their sandwiches kick ass. In fact, I was eating one of their sandwiches when my ceiling collapsed. (The fact that I finished it amidst the rubble is the best recommendation I can give.)

The place in the Laundromat (next to Rush Hour): This

anything. A couple of years ago, the service was fucking horrendous there. You would order an iced coffee and it would be like a cup of warm coffee with one ice cube in it, served by an emaciated hipster in a bad mood. However, the décor was nice with paintings of Pegasus on the walls and a little theater in the back. Also, you could loiter there for hours, writing or gabbing. It was also the most flyer-laden spot in all of NY. Sometimes, when I would get lonely or badly needed to promote a show, I would put a few flyers in my bag and just sit in the Pee Pony waiting for a friend to walk in. It almost never failed. Then the inevitable happened—The Pee Pony was sold to French people. Previously, it had been owned by the woman who owns Max Fish, and I heard that she owned it basically because it served as a fire exit to Max Fish but that she really didn't give a crap about it, which could explain the crappy iced coffee and stale muffins. But the French people actually cared about the taste of the food and the service! The obvious bonus of this change in ownership is the fact that the food got much better and more varied and the service is great now (I only say that because the waitress told me she loves my column.) The negative side of this is that the lovely paintings of Pegasus have now been replaced by paintings of Rimbaud and other French shit. (I love Rimbaud but I don't want to look at him while I'm eating.)

Also, it is no longer possible to sit there for ten hours nursing one cup of tea because now people actually wait for tables there.

Le Pere Pinard (Ludlow between Houston & Stanton): When I first saw that a French bistro was opening on Ludlow Street, I put my head in my hands and wept. "It's all over," I thought. What had once been a dirty bodega that sold Slim Jims and 24 oz. Budweisers was now a fancy pants bistro. I was simply not prepared. However, shortly after my appendix ruptured (due to the medical experts at Saint Vincent's or

Chapter Fifteen
Miscellaneous

Pickles: Out of all the questions I get asked on a daily basis at my job, none is more common than, "Do you know where Guss' Pickles is?" **Guss' Pickles** (87 Orchard St.) is a famed pickle store, which was once run by a man named Izzy Gus, but today is run by a fellow named Tim Baker who has been plying the pickle trade since he was sixteen. Out of all the pickles I've known in my lifetime, none are tastier or more potent than Guss' pickles, and that could explain why people are frigging mad for them. On Sundays, I can look out my window and actually see a line of people a block away, waiting to buy pickles even when it's freezing or raining out. Guss' Pickles used to be on Essex Street but they got the boot when their landlord decided to condominium-ize their building. Do not, whatever you do go to "The Pickle Guys" on Essex Street. They are a sad rip-off of Guss', and although they "pretend" to know the recipes, they don't—pure and simple.

Candy: If you have a sweet tooth or are caught in the throes of PMS, you should consider heading over to **Economy Candy** (Rivington between Ludlow & Essex) where you can find everything from Pop Rocks to tootsie rolls by the pound. They also sell sugar free candy and little chocolates shaped like crosses.

The Pink Pony or the "Pee Pony" (Ludlow between Houston & Stanton): I used to refer to the Pink Pony as the "Pee Pony" because it was one of the only places where you could stealthily use the bathroom without actually buying

Photo: Kat Fasano

dogs, pastrami sandwiches and the like. Katz's has been there forever so it's very popular with tourists, and sometimes it's too crowded.

However, occasionally you'll find that a table and chair have been laid out at Hot Bagels (but it's usually only one table and three chairs) and this presents one with the option of actually hanging out at Hot Bagels as though it were a bar or restaurant. And, because there is usually only one table, this makes Hot Bagels something of an exclusive bar/restaurant. For a while, I tried to make Hot Bagels the "hip place to be" by hanging out at the one table with my friend, Bruce, while drinking a 24 oz. which I had acquired from Hot Bagels' cooler. It didn't really catch on, although I found sitting there at 3 am and watching drunks stumble in after a night of bar-hopping, to be one of the most entertaining activities to date, and I plan on going back maybe this week, although they have been hiding the table more and more.

There is always a very lively atmosphere at Hot Bagels although one of the guys who works there is a dick, and it's really hard to make him smile. The other employees are quite nice. Hot Bagels also serves little cakes, canolis and cookies. The cookies, especially the mysterious "diet cookies" are dry and will crumble all over you. The only real exception is the "black and white" cookie, which is bigger than my head, and quite tasty.

Go to Hot Bagels for a donut, a black and white cookie, a little piece of cake, a cup of tea or a 24 oz. can of Budweiser, but more than anything, go there for the atmosphere!

Next to Hot Bagels is **Katz's Deli** (205 E. Houston), which could be defined quite aptly as a vegetarian's worst nightmare. You will smell Katz's long before it ever comes into your line of vision. It smells like a giant hot dog that got left in a giant microwave for too long and has now exploded all over the corner of Houston and Ludlow. In the window of Katz's you'll see giant sausages hanging from hooks alongside letters to Katz's from politicians like Ronald Reagan thanking Katz's for sending them salamis. Once inside, you'll find a potpourri of heart attack-inducing meat and potato products like knishes, hot

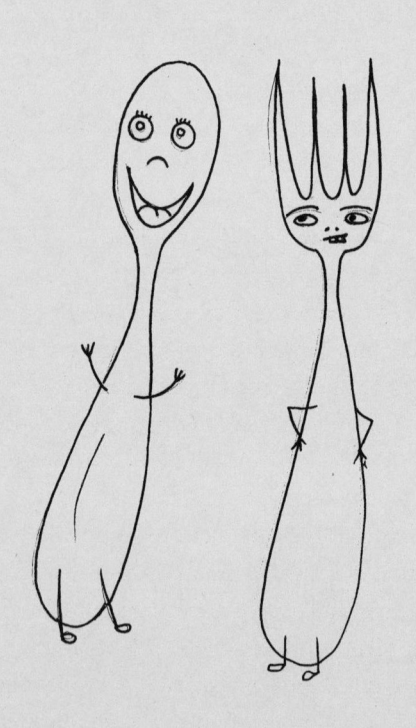

Next to Bereket is an empty store for rent, which would make an excellent troll museum, but which I unfortunately, cannot afford.

Next to that is **Pomme Pomme** (123 2nd Ave.) a Belgian fry joint, where you can also get "strips of fire" (really spicy chicken fingers), popcorn shrimp and other deep fried snacks. The fries here are so grease-laden that they are heavy to hold. This might actually curb any negative effects of the fries on one's health because they also (much like the 40 oz. Budweiser) incorporate a workout.

Next to the fry place is a newspaper stand, which also sells an assortment of energy bars, candy and soda. Next to The Newspaper Place is Ray's Pizza, which I covered Chapter Six.

Next to Ray's is **Yoshi** (201 E. Houston), a Japanese restaurant, which is pretty decent and reasonably priced. However, they don't open till 5 and they don't stay open too late so the window of time in which one can eat there is very limited.

Next to Yoshi is **Hot Bagels** (203 E. Houston) which may in fact not even be called "Hot Bagels" but there is a giant sign, with letters that look like they have flames bursting off of them that says, "Hot Bagels" on the front of this establishment so that if you say, "I'm going to Hot Bagels," to someone, they will automatically know where you are going. The bagels at Hot Bagels sort of suck though. They are kind of stale, which is less noticeable if you get them toasted, but otherwise, I'd recommend maybe going for a donut. However, if like a former roommate of mine, you stumble by Hot Bagels at 6 am every morning on your way home from the gay sex club, you will undoubtedly find that their bagels are fresh and hot.

Hot Bagels is more of a deli where you can order a cup of coffee or get a six-pack of beer or soda, than a restaurant where one sits down to eat and drink.

Chapter Fourteen
The Food Court

If one were to liken the Lower East Side to a shopping mall, the area on the South Side of Houston Street, between Orchard and Ludlow, would be the "food court."

At the corner of Houston and Orchard lies **Bereket Turkish Kebab House** (187 E. Houston) a wonderfully inexpensive, Middle Eastern joint, which is open 24 hours a day. The place is brightly lit, and the tables are close together, but the falafels ($3) are tasty as are the kebabs and baklava. There never seems to be a time when Bereket isn't packed, but the line moves fast.

On summer weekends, usually around 3 in the morning, one can dine at Bereket while simultaneously enjoying the live sounds of Saint Brad Prowley, the only canonized saint in the Hal religion. Brad Prowley who is also known as "the karaoke man" can be found directly in front of Bereket, singing into the microphone of his boom box, a "Lasonic Jumbo" which operates on ten batteries. At first glance Saint Brad doesn't look like a classic soul vocalist. His baggy green trousers are cinched by a makeshift, rope belt. His coke bottle glasses are loosely held together by tape, and his bowl-cut hair is both the color and texture of straw. His ill-fitting polyester shirt, which is emblazoned with an image of a disco-dancing John Travolta, is riddled in holes. Brad looks more like Willard from the movie Willard, than an R&B superstar, but when he pops in a tape and begins singing classics like "Let's get it on," "Mrs. Jones" and "Cloud Nine" even the most jaded LES residents stop in their tracks. Brad will make your meal at Bereket completely unforgettable.

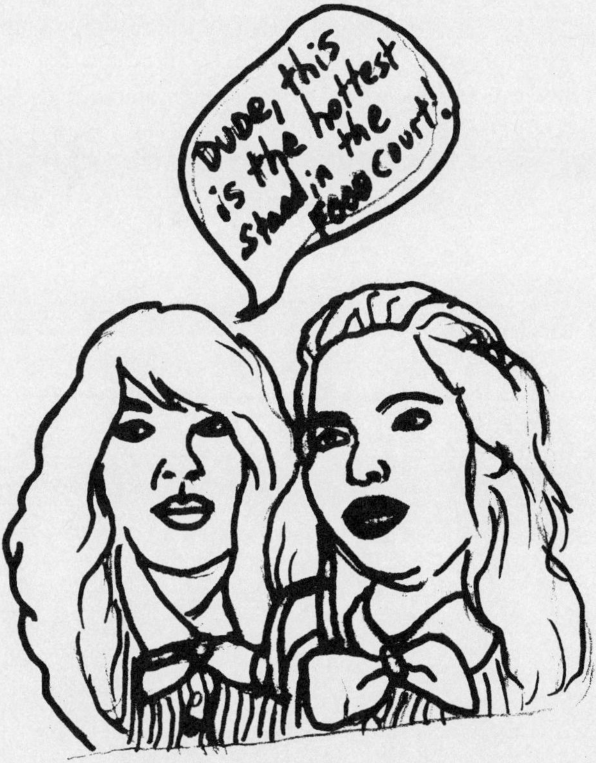
Dude, this is the hottest stand in the FOOD court!

sage from another diner while munching on a greasy omelet. A&A has excellent fries and hot dogs, and in the morning they serve up fresh donuts.

Right smack in the middle of these delis is **Off Track Betting**, where everyday, hundreds of Chuck Bukowski-types (only without the literary fame) gather in an effort to reap their fortunes through gambling. Because gambling is the only vice that doesn't interest me, I have never been inside of OTB. What I can tell you is that if you are flirting with the notion of a gambling addiction, you should, by all means, stop into OTB, where you might find that the environment is actually a deterrent from delving any further into the abyss of gambling.

session of gambling. If you stop into the Olympic, you are sure to bear witness to several loud arguments between an extremely vocal staff and their loitering customers. You will also get to hear melodramatic soliloquies by Olympic regulars. Because this establishment serves beer and is open 24 hours a day, it really is the premiere after hours club on the LES, however, when it comes to eating food here, I would recommend sticking to things that are really hard to fuck up like a grilled cheese or cereal. The service is horrible here, and you may be tempted to dine and dash after waiting twenty minutes for your check, but the staff here will come after you (especially if you do it in a monkey costume, which I unfortunately tried). However, once they nab you, they will simply ask for the money you owe them and then let you go.

On the southwest corner of Delancey and Essex, next to the subway station, you will find **America's Choice Deli** (111 Delancey St.), a good place to get a sandwich, a cup of coffee or Entenmann's products. The service is friendly, although it's often a little too friendly, and if you go there often enough, and you are a woman, you will invariably be asked out on a date. America's Choice is equipped with a lotto machine, which is a good thing if you have a dollar and a dream, but a bad thing if the jackpot is up to twenty million, and all you want to do is get a cup of coffee and get the Hell out. When the lotto jackpot soars, the entirety of OTB finds it's way to America's Choice where they torture the staff by giving them extremely complex directions for printing out their lotto tickets. If you are in the mood for a bagel, I recommend skipping America's Choice and heading over instead to **Happiness Deli** (101 Delancey St.), where they have fresh H&H bagels delivered each morning, and where you can also get a quick cup of joe or a sandwich. A couple doors down is **A&A deli** (95 Delancey St.), one of the more sad eating establishments on Delancey. The attitude here is laid back, so much so that it's not uncommon to see a shirtless diner receiving a back masin color combinations, which you never thought anyone would ever put together. (Authors Note: While I have purchased many items at Rainbow, I hand-wash all of them as they tend to fall apart upon coming into contact with a washing machine.)

On the North side of Delancey, you'll also find several fast-food places including Subway, Wendy's, McDonald's, Burger King and a Taco Bell / KFC combo. All of these places are packed, the food is heart-attack-inducing, and the service is a nightmare, but when you're broke, you really can't argue with a bean burrito from Taco Bell, not to mention the Taco Bell can also be quite entertaining if you're in the mood to watch a crack head try to figure out how to use the soda machine.

If you are health conscious or if you have heard one too many urban legends about people finding rats' tails in their Taco Bell, your prospects of finding food on the LES are rather limited. I used to think that you had to cross Houston Street in order to get a piece of fruit in this city, but then I discovered **The Essex Street Market** (120 Essex St.) on Essex and Delancey, where several vendors have set up shops, which offer a wide variety of fruits and vegetables. There is also a smoothie stand, two fresh fish stands, a stand that sells Goya products, a Chinese dumpling stand and a stand that sells religious wares like Jesus candles and "Go Away Evil Cologne." The Essex Street Market certainly isn't fancy, but it really is the only place to get fresh fruit and fish in the hood, unless you are willing to head over to Chinatown where you can acquire these things in abundance.

Directly across the street from The Essex Street Market, on the south side of Delancey is **The Olympic Restaurant** (115 Delancey St.), a place more notable for its ambience than for its food. The Olympic is small, with something like only seven tables and a counter, but it is lively, and it is a favorite hangout of OTB regulars, who need to refuel for yet another

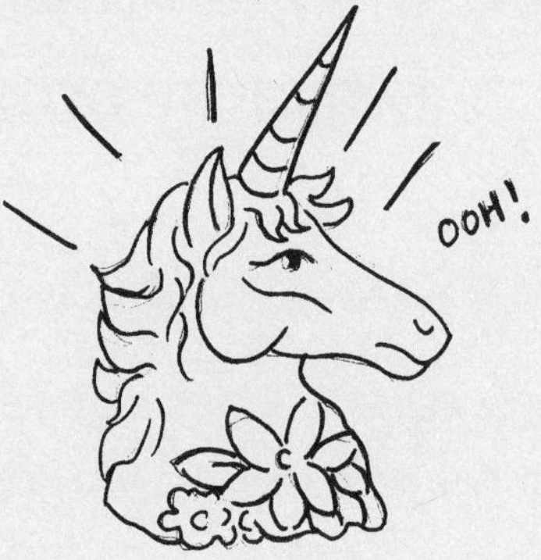
OOH!

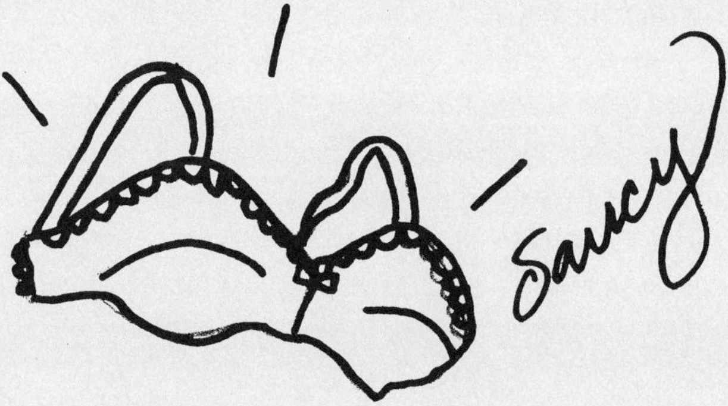
Saucy

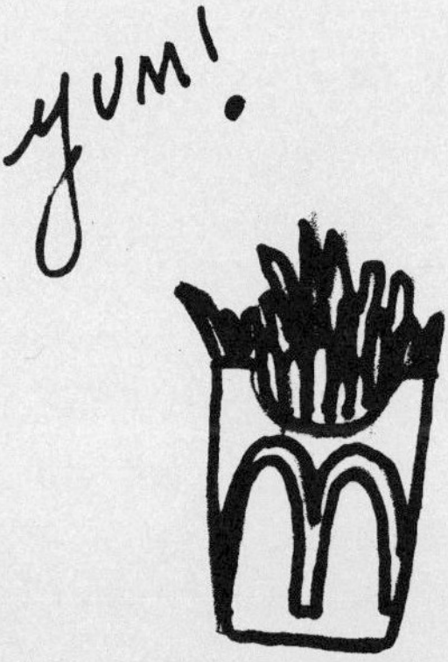
yum!

Chapter Thirteen
Delancey Street

Delancey Street is a big street, which is named after a dead rich guy named James Delancey, who had his property taken away after the American Revolution because he was a British sympathizer. Despite this, he still has his own street, a street lined with fast-food joints, a liquor store, a 99-cent store, an Off Track Betting and many other fine establishments, which I'm sure would make him proud.

My fave store on the North side of Delancey Street is **Gem Home Stores** (128 Delancey St.). You can get everything in this joint: candy, towels, fans, pillows, fountains, holographic portraits of the Virgin Mary, mesh baseball caps and porcelain statuettes of unicorns. (There are many stores like this one on Clinton Street between Delancey and Rivington, but none are quite as good.) A couple doors down from Gem, you'll find **Secret Outlet Lingerie** a store, which sells cheap underwear often of the racy variety. They also sell tights for only 99-cents. (Make sure you don't accidentally pick up kid's tights.) There are several cheap shoe stores along this stretch, where one can acquire go-go boots for less than 20 dollars. A little further west from Gem you'll find **Rainbow** a delightful women's clothier where one can pick up obscenely slutty dresses, miniskirts, shoes, tops and underwear,

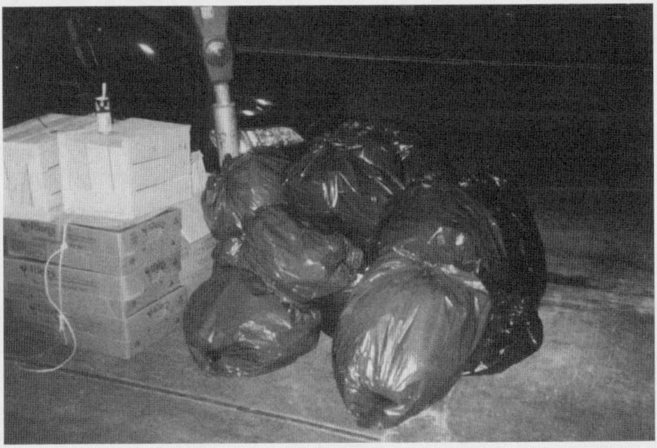

fabulous prizes and giveaways like pocket-sized containers of water-based lube, and "pocket-rocket" vibrators. (Of course, on the day when I had to pick up the two giant bags of lube and vibrators for the party, every man and woman in the Western Hemisphere happened to be in the store. Now, there's really nothing too embarrassing about carrying one, maybe two vibrators out of a store, but 40 tends to lend itself to neighborhood gossip.)

Perhaps the most notable thing about Toys is their unbelievable selection of vibrators. Hello Kitty-shaped, Tiki-doll-shaped, polar bear-shaped; you name it, this store's got it! Toys also sells fun stuff like wrist and ankle cuffs, liquid latex, wacky condoms, and implements of torture like riding crops and paddles. There is also a whole rack of unusual pornography there, including my favorite comic book, "Fetish Fairies" and there is a whole library of porn movies for rent. However, if you have a book to write (as I do) I highly recommend not buying any of these items because you will find it extremely hard to get anything done at all.

The sexperts who work at Toys are so comfortable with talking about sex that they make others more comfortable, and this provides shoppers with a pleasant experience.

---

9. *Lord of the Cockrings* is the story of "Scroto Baggins" a computer programmer from Secaucus, NJ, who is magically transported to Middle Earth after purchasing a mysterious cockring at Toys in Babeland. In Middle Earth, Scroto meets "Rosebudweiser" a magical fairy who tells him that he must dispose of the deadly cockring by pitching it into the fires of Mount Doom where it was forged. Adventure ensues! Said film was written by me and directed by Nick Zedd during December of 2001.

claims it was easy for him and his lady-friend to sneak into a booth together, despite the signs which indicated that this was not allowed.

Face also mentioned that this friendly establishment sells "VCR Head Cleaner" which apparently, people use as poppers or "rush," although I don't know if this is true, so don't snort VCR Head Cleaner and then sue me when you end up in the hospital.

There is also a porn magazine shop on Delancey between Essex and Norfolk where one can pick up a copy of Juggs or Big Butt and a lotto ticket and soda, although I can't imagine that perusing porn in this busy environment could be relaxing or enjoyable in any way. I suppose if you know exactly what you want, and you don't have to stop and browse, this is a good place to get your wares.

One porn shop, which is not just a porn shop, but a sex superstore, which I LOVE, is **Toys In Babeland** (942 Rivington St.). If I were a millionaire, I know for a fact that I would individually support this store for the fiscal year every year. Toys In Babeland is run by women and is manned by women seven days a week. The women who work at Toys are not mere clerks, they are Sexperts, and they are more than happy to answer a wide array of questions that shoppers might have when searching for a new dildo, butt plug, bullwhip or "personal massager." They even hold monthly seminars on subjects like female ejaculation and anal sex, and they have an informative web site where you can learn fun facts about sex.

I am particularly fond of Toys after they allowed me to film the first scene of *Lord of the Cockrings* there.[9] It was hard to concentrate on making a movie when there was so much fun stuff around, like nipple suction cups, which I noticed the cast and crew seemed to enjoy sticking to their foreheads. Toys was also generous enough to sponsor the first annual "Shout Magazine Administrative Assistants Day Extravaganza" where several oppressed administrative assistants went home with

Chapter Twelve
Where To Get Porn and Other Potentially Embarrassing Stuff

I really like porn, but I am too embarrassed to buy or rent it. The only time I ever rented porn, it was John Wayne Bobbit's *Uncut* from Kim's Video (on Avenue A), and I almost had a coronary when it got stuck in my VCR. Eventually, I wrenched it out of the clutches of said VCR, unscathed, but vowed to never again tempt fate by renting such foul porn. Most of my porn has been given to me by Faceboy, which means that most of my porn is comical and/or disturbing, and most often it features midgets or mustached dudes from the seventies, which means that it's not all entirely "jackable."

When a nameless porn shop opened on Essex Street between Delancey and Rivington it was cause for celebration amongst art stars, many of whom are vocal, enthusiastic fans of porn. Faceboy impresses me in that he has no qualms about purchasing porn. Therefore, I thought he would be the perfect consultant for this section of my travel guide. In the name of providing you, the reader, with an accurate portrait of this new porn vendor, I interviewed Face over a couple (ten) tall boys, about his experience (or experiences) there.

"Well, for starters, I didn't spend too much time there, but I was there long enough to see that they had a great selection, including modern, sleazy, hardcore and classics like *Deep Throat*," he began. He went on to explain that this new shop has "booths" which one can go into in order to view porn privately. In most booth-equipped shops, couples are not allowed to enter the booths together. However, at this shop, Face

Photo: Kat Fasano

Chapter Eleven
Where to Make Copies

If you are a masochist, but don't have five hundred dollars to pay a dominatrix to torture you, I highly recommend going to Kinkos where the staff will torture you for only a few dollars. The Houston Street Kinkos is like no other when it comes to ruining your day. I like to call this Kinkos the "Ghetto Kinkos" because nothing there works and because everything there (scissors, stapler…) is chained to the tables. The place is also grossly understaffed so that the simple act of getting change in order to use the self-service copier can take upwards of an hour. In fact, I have had so many negative experiences making flyers at Kinkos that I am planning on making flyers that say, "Kinkos Sucks" and handing them out to people.

However, as with every cloud, this one has a silver lining! It is extremely easy to steal from the Ghetto Kinkos. And, I highly recommend stealing as much as possible. If you see a glue stick, put it in your bag. Pens, white-out, staples…they are yours, free, with your special five-finger discount. Bring a big backpack.

Because the Kinkos "team members" don't pay attention to customers, it is quite easy to simply walk out without paying! Although, if you go there almost every day, like I do, it isn't wise to walk out too often. Conversely, the turnover rate of team members is so high that if you steal one week and then return the next, you will find a whole new set of employees who have never seen you and don't know what you're up to.

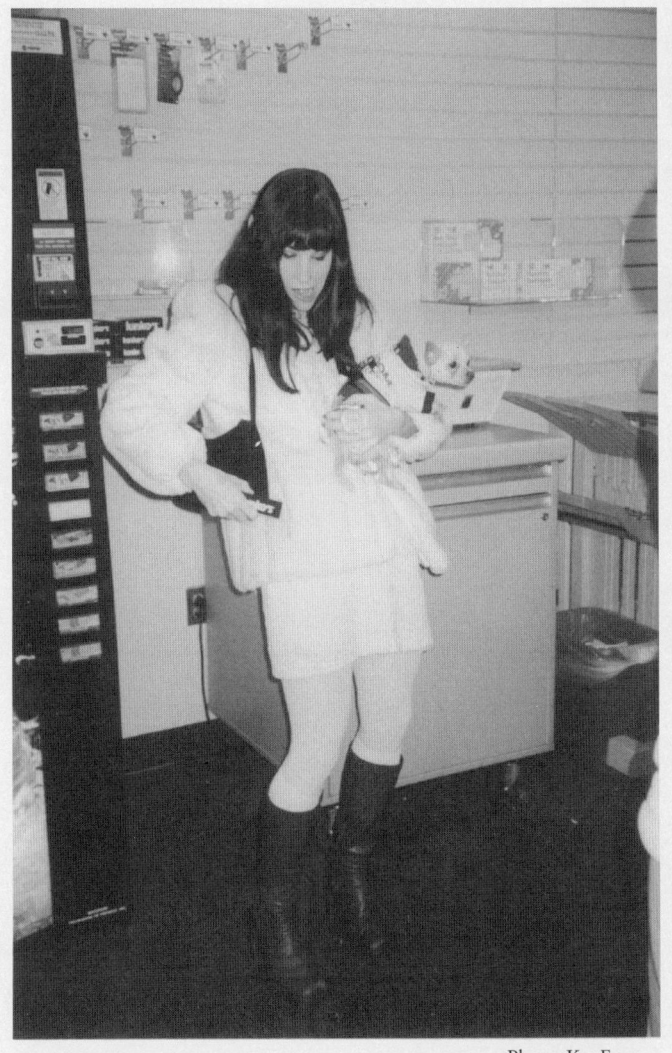

Photo: Kat Fasano

There are plenty of other Mexican dining establishments on the LES, but I have never eaten in them. Many Mexican restaurants on the LES have basically the same stuff. If you're not sure what to get, it's really hard to fuck up rice and beans. Beer is also good and provides you with carbohydrates.

Photo: Kat Fasano

ages can be ordered "to go." The only drawback to the Hat is that, more often than not, the service is slow. (I know several people who have dined and dashed because they just couldn't wait around for their check any longer.)

2. Tres Aztecas (corner of Rivington & Allen)

Tres is less crowded than the Hat, and the service is faster, but it doesn't have the same excellent view that the Hat has. (The Hat's glass windows look out onto Ludlow Street, where you can sit and people watch for hours (while you wait for your check). And, Tres Aztecas looks out onto ugly-ass Allen Street.) Again, the portions are large, the salsa is hot and the margaritas are strong. On Sundays the place is filled with extremely drunk people who have been boozing since church.

3. El Nuevo Amanacer (117 Stanton)

When I attempt to go the Hat, and it's too packed, I tend to cross the street, and go here. This is an excellent, quiet spot, perfect for anyone who wants to get away from the crowd. El Nuevo used to be open 24 hours a day, which was fantastic. When the bars gave my friends and I the boot at 4:30, we would hop over to this joint and continue drinking, but those days are gone. Today, El Nuevo is open only till about 2. Many of the treats here are coated in several hundred layers of cheese, including the "Mexican pizza" which is like a hardened disc of cheese that you could play Frisbee with.

5. Castillo de Agua (113 Rivington)

This actually isn't a Mexican restaurant at all, but a Dominican restaurant, although many of the dishes are similar. Salsa music blares, as neighborhood locals scream over tables to one another. The fried chicken is rockin' but the coffee is scary.

Chapter Ten
Mexican Food

If you're like me, there's nothing you like more than first dousing your tongue in burning hot salsa and then putting out the fire with an ice-cold margarita, and then following this sadomasochistic ritual with a gigantic burrito. If you're in the mood for Mexican, you're in luck! There are a number of classy, Mexican joints strewn about the LES, where you can gorge yourself on phat Mexican food.

1. El Sombrero or "The Hat" (corner of Ludlow & Stanton)
While scientists have discovered things like how to clone animals and grow a human ear on the back of a rat, one burning question in the field of science remains unanswered: What is in those damn margaritas? I have heard everything from grain alcohol to crack cocaine, but one thing is certain—you should NEVER drink one on an empty stomach. These famed margaritas draw crowds from near and far, and that's why I recommend if you're planning on dining at the Hat, get there early (sixish) or late (twelvish). The food is filling, and if you do eat a whole burrito before going out, don't expect to be able to move for several hours. Often, when I dine at the Hat, I go for something lighter, like rice and beans. The food is tasty, but I wouldn't recommend getting a fajita, especially if you're sitting near someone who has asthma (unless you hate them). The fajitas tend to completely "smoke out" the entire restaurant in a matter of seconds. If you're with a big crowd you'll be happy to know that pitchers of margaritas are available. Or, if you're running errands, or maybe jogging over to the East River, you'll be delighted to know that these tasty frozen bever-

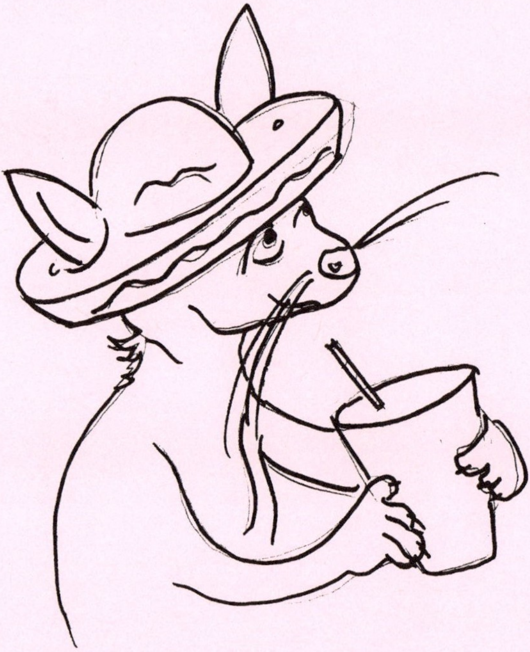

BYOB and nudity is encouraged.

There are plenty of other open mikes in town, which I don't go to because I can only devote two nights a week to my open mike addiction, but if you go to either the Anti-Slam or Faceboy's open mike, the regulars there, who are serious open mike addicts, will point you in the right direction.

But, I honestly wasn't surprised when many art stars showed up. (And, if you want proof of America's failing security, it's in the fact that Anti-Slam regular, Francis McNerdz, was able to get past the police checkpoint on Houston Street, with a plastic knife in his pocket by simply saying, "I'm going to the Anti-Slam!") People expressed vastly different viewpoints. Some people were all for a war, some were completely against retaliation; some people thought we should let the mob take care of it. Christopher Brodeur thought we should rebuild the towers exactly as they were, but turn them into 220 stories of low-income housing. Mike Amato thought we should build the towers exactly as they were, only underground. People spoke of missing relatives and narrow escapes, but it was a drunken poet named Pablo whose words stuck with me the most. "Look at what a handful of destructive minds can do," he said, "Now imagine what a handful of creative, beautiful minds can do."

There are people who come to the Anti-Slam, and then they either start to get successful or they start to get laid so they stop coming, and whenever I run into these people, they always thank Faceboy and me for giving them the opportunity to be heard when no one else would, but I always feel that I should be thanking them. Any art star who has ever done anything at my open mike, whether it's pulling an onion out of their vagina or doing a Steely Dan cover has given me real faith in life, liberty and the pursuit of happiness. As long as people can still insert produce into bodily orifices on stage at the Anti-Slam, I will continue to live in this country. The art stars have taught me more than I learned in four years of college (I did go to art school) and have made me laugh harder than I did watching Jack Tripper as a child. I know that no matter what happens in my life—personal disasters, loss of lovers, loss of organs, loss of pets, national crises, even war, the Anti-Slam will continue to rock!

The Anti-Slam will always be only three dollars. It is

missing. I broke down in front of my doorstep. Even though everyone in my building whispered about my elf ears, called me a witch, and gossiped about my freaky troll museum, he was always friendly to me, always smiled at me, and now I would never see him smile again because I knew as so many New Yorkers did that most of the "missing" signs were really death pronouncements. I walked to the bodega to get beer. (I had been planning on getting tea, but beer now seemed more apropos. Unfortunately for the Taliban, the attack only served to double the amount of drinking, promiscuous sex and debauchery in America.) When I crossed Delancey, I saw trucks carrying the National Guard crossing the Williamsburg Bridge. Suddenly, I felt what people in other countries have probably been feeling for centuries—the feeling that nothing would last—that I was in a war zone.

Less than 24 hours after the attack, television news programs and newspapers developed catchy graphics and slogans like "America Under Attack" and "America Rising" with which to contain their war propaganda. Newscasters repeatedly aired maudlin interviews with grieving family members over and over again. Americans gathered around their televisions like zombies, with their arms spread out to the second altar, flicking the sacred remote, searching for answers. Out on the street I saw no one. I wanted to scream, "Where are all the people?" At the very least, people should have been out, drinking themselves to numbness.

I decided to host the Anti-Slam that Wednesday night, the 12th. Maybe one person would show up, and even worse, maybe that one person would be a stand-up comic from Hackensack, who was just jonesing for some stage stage time in order to "tighten-up" their set for Stand Up NY, but that would still be one person, one person who believed in what they had to say enough to say it in front of others, who wasn't staring at CBS (the only channel most of us could get) with glazed eyeballs.

who was a regular at the Anti-Slam (pre-rehab), and got his wallet back, but it was missing twenty bucks! I also occasionally add a "no hurling chairs" rule, as certain art stars have been known to hurl chairs for shits and giggles, and I am always the one who has to do the explaining at the end of the night, when several chairs are missing legs. Before the show begins, I remind everyone, "Don't be dicks. Say it in six." Or even better, "Don't be a whore. Say it in four," in order to encourage everyone to stay within the 6-minute time limit.

If you do decide to attend the Wednesday or Sunday night open mike night, be prepared to witness anything and everything. You will never hear me utter the phrase, "I have seen it all," because just when I think I've seen it all, I see a man gallop onto the stage in a Speedo, and proceed to explain Hegel while simultaneously pouring baking soda and vinegar into his Speedo, forming a children's science fair-like volcanic explosion to occur within his swimsuit, which will then begin to seep out of the tiny holes in the Speedo's fabric, and explode on the stage, causing the first row of audience members to run in terror. No, I have not seen everything, but I have seen a woman paint a penis onto canvas with her menstrual blood and a man paint his penis purple. I have cried, laughed, been driven to nausea and been inspired.

The art stars at the open mike have become my extended family, a family of schizophrenics, drunks, and bipolar interpretive dancers. Seven years ago when I started the open mike, I would think, "I don't want to be a 50-year old open mike host," but in that time, my ideas about "success" have changed dramatically. Now I consider every week the Anti-Slam continues a success.

The morning after the Sept. 11th attack on the World Trade Center, there were no people on the streets and the smell of rubble, burning and dead bodies was in the air. I remember that Wednesday morning I left my building and saw a poster with my next-door neighbor's face on it. He was

building that had formerly been a brothel, which fronted as a tailor shop named "Cucho Taylor" which was located at 145 Ludlow Street, an area, which at the time was even more heinous than 2nd Street and Ave. B.

I decided to hold the Anti-Slam on Wednesday nights, opposite the popular Nuyorican Poet's Café slam. I also offered double the stage time (six minutes as opposed to three) for almost half the price (three dollars as opposed to five). I modeled my open mike after *Faceboy's Open Mike*, and it became something of a spin-off of Faceboy's show. (One might call it the "*Joanie Loves Chachi*" to his "*Happy Days*.")

Both of our shows have three main rules; no heckling the performer, no assaulting the audience and no trashing the space. (Considering the fact that the original Collective burned down, this third rule is extremely important. Still, there are often art stars who have the misguided notion that they are Pete Townsend, and so they attempt to trash the stage.) Recently, a nude art star ran his spread out buttocks along the mike stand, and I was not quite sure if this was a transgression of rule #3, nevertheless, I ran to the kitchen and returned with Windex, which I used to carefully clean the violated mike stand.

Under the influence of alcohol, I occasionally add extra rules to my show. For two years, no one was allowed to insult John Tesh (star of *Entertainment Tonight* and solo recording star), and I have no idea why I brought this rule into existence, but then an art star did a whole set about how they'd been an intern on Letterman and they met John Tesh, and described him as being a major asshole, and I was forced to drop my John Tesh rule. Now people can insult John Tesh as much as they want! I also added a "no mugging the audience" (and I don't mean Mr. Firley-style mugging, I mean actually stealing money) rule after one art star, who claimed to be doing a conceptual performance piece, mugged an audience member named Frank. Frank eventually tracked down the perpetrator,

party" at his apartment after the show. I was so nervous! He was so cool! However, when I got to the party, what I found was Faceboy and his friend, Jeff, sitting by themselves drinking. No one else had come to his party. That's when I realized he was an alienated freak, just like me! After that, Faceboy and I became inseparable friends.

It wasn't long before Face suggested I start my own open mike, but it wasn't until I ventured into a "poetry slam" that I found a real reason to start one. (The origins of the Anti-Slam are explained in-depth in my book, *Sex Symbol for the Insane*, so I won't go into too much detail here.) The poetry slam is a phenomenon wherein poets take the mike, much like they would at any old open mike, and read their stuff. However, at the end of their set, they are judged by three judges, on a scale of one to ten like figure skaters or gymnasts. Because of the competitive nature of the slam, very few writers took chances, and all of the poetry started to sound the same because it was suited to please. There was no room for failure, no room for experimentation. The pretentiousness of the whole thing ate away at me, and so I decided to start fucking with the poetry slam. I did this in several ways. I would become a judge one night, and give everyone a ten thus screwing up the system. Another night, I made fart noises into the mike for my entire set.

Faceboy pointed out the fact that by going to the Wednesday night slam week after week, I was contributing financially to the slam's success. Together we brainstormed a better way to combat the growing popularity of the slam, and eventually we conjured up a healthy alternative to the pompous nature of poetry slams everywhere; *Reverend Jen's Anti-Slam*, a kinder, gentler, lard-free, open mike, where everyone would receive a ten no matter what. I would even select three judges each week, whose job it would be to shout, "Ten!" after every performance.

It was decided that my open mike would be held at the new Collective Unconscious, which had been rebuilt in a

I'll never forget my first open mike. I was wearing purple pants and a fake fur jacket, and I wandered in eating a Snickers bar. It was January 1995, and it was freezing cold. It was at the old Collective Unconscious, and they had no heat. (Faceboy's Sunday night open mike used to take place at Collective Unconscious, which was located on Avenue B and 2nd Street, up until April of 1995 when it was destroyed by a blazing inferno, and Faceboy moved his open mike to Surf Reality.) A beatific man at the door collected three dollars from me and told me it was their "Con Ed Benefit Night." I approached the show's host, "Faceboy," a bald headed, handsome young man, and asked him if I could perform. He asked me my name, and having recently been ordained, I told him, "Reverend Jen." I was something like last on the list, but I sat in the audience completely transfixed by the art stars who graced the "stage." (There was actually no stage at all, just a microphone.) These weren't like the fake freaks in art school who repelled up the walls of the sculpture building and masturbated at the top because they saw Matthew Barney do something similar. These were the true freaks, the people who were making art because they had to. This is where art went. It was like walking into a dream.

I went home that night and tried to sleep, but I couldn't. My head was racing with ideas. I could go there every week! No one could tell me I couldn't perform there. No one could tell me my shit was too weird or too kitsch. The open mike presented me with freedom, and an outlet for my ideas. Had I not discovered it when I did, I would probably have joined a cult or developed a drug habit.

I became a regular at Faceboy's show, and I began to worship Faceboy, considering him the coolest person alive. One week he announced that he needed a stage manager for a play he was directing, and I shot my hand in the air like Arnold Horshack on speed. I took the helm as stage manager and almost peed myself when Faceboy invited me to a "cast

Chapter Nine
Open Mikes

Nothing beats cheap entertainment, and nothing is cheaper and more entertaining than the two greatest open mikes in the history of Western Civilization: *Faceboy's Open Mike* on Sunday nights at **Surf Reality** (172 Allen Street) and *Reverend Jen's Anti-Slam* on Wednesday nights at **Collective Unconscious** (145 Ludlow Street).

In 1995, after my band, Pop Rox, broke up, I was extremely depressed and desperately needed a place to express myself in front of others. When a friend of mine directed me to Faceboy's open mike, I not only found a place to perform, but I also found a group of like-minded freaks, who were bursting with energy to create, and who also desperately needed to express themselves in front of others. I found my church.

At first, I was wary. I half expected to wander into a room filled with bongo-playing, finger-snapping poets who, in an attempt to appear cool, were regressing to a much cooler era, by emulating the poetry-reading style of Kerouac and Ginsburg. (I believe they call them "Wanna-Beatniks.") But, I wanted to progress, even if it meant facing the fact that my own era is totally uncool. All my life, people have been saying, "Dude, you should have been born thirty years earlier." And, yes, I am sure things would have been pretty groovy in the sixties, and there would have been a lot of LSD and other drugs, and a lot of beautiful dudes with long hair, and a lot of free love, and a spirit of protest, but I feel it is my duty to take this sucky era in which I live, in which fat jocks turn over pretzel trucks at Wigstock, and transform it into something beautiful. I want to make art for the present in the present.

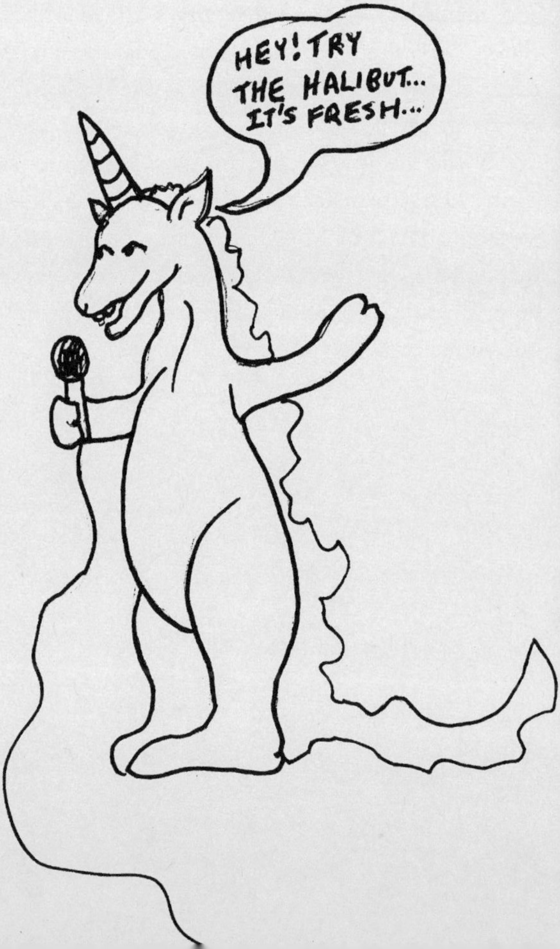
HEY! TRY THE HALIBUT... IT'S FRESH...

wonder of trolls.

(I also must admit I was very drunk when I decided to open a Troll Museum in my apartment. But, I was sober when I constructed the museum, and I guess that's what matters.)

In any case, The Troll Museum offers viewers a break from the daily grind, and it also offers a break from more formal museums, where visitors are often made to feel inferior for not quite "getting it." In his book, Offbeat Museums, writer, Saul Rubin, explains, "The dawn of the 20th century marked a sobering period for America's exhibit halls. Museums were increasingly perceived as solemn places designed to educate the public in a somber manner, a concept that persists today. America's most cherished institutions are marble-lined mausoleums, presided over by high-minded boards of trustees and guarded by uniformed sentinels armed with attendance clickers." Having once worked as a guard at The Met, I can relate all too well. That is why at the Troll Museum, our guards are allowed to drink and smoke on the job.

If you are looking for the most authentic and slightly insane LES experience that there is, I cannot recommend a visit to the LES Troll Museum enough, and I am not just saying that because I am the head curator. It is open by appointment only. (Because I still have a day job.) For an appointment, call our hotline at (212)560-7235.

goal, as head curator to conceive praiseworthy exhibitions. I didn't have to look far for inspiration when I laid eyes upon the "Armani Retrospective" at the Guggenheim last winter. Weeks later, I contacted Armani, and learned that all along, he had been secretly designing couture for troll dolls! I was ecstatic, and immediately offered him a retrospective, which he graciously accepted. "Armani at The Troll Museum" drew record-breaking crowds, and gained us recognition that I never thought possible.

Despite this, many people still deign to ask, "Reverend Jen, why is that you sacrificed your living room in order to build a troll museum?" For starters, I never used my living room. (Living rooms are used for "vegging" an activity that is foreign to me, the world's most prolific art star.) Secondly, I noticed a dearth of Troll Museums on the Lower East Side, and I also noticed a dearth of fun LES activities, which were not directly related to sex, drugs and rock-n-roll. Thirdly, while trolls have always fascinated me, it seems that many people take them for granted. I wanted to take the seemingly banal troll out of its everyday context and put it in an environment where its extraordinary qualities would be exemplified. I wanted to amaze people, to show them wonder and magic, in an age where such things seem only to belong to the sunken city of Atlantis. I don't believe in Santa Claus or even God, but I do believe that a sense of wonder can still exist, even for cynical, black turtleneck-sporting atheists like me! (I know it's a bit heavy for a chapter on trolls, but stick with me.) We live in an age when the men who are considered magicians are really only skilled tricksters who are capable of slight of hand tricks that befuddle normal human beings. I wanted to be a real magician. That is why I opened my museum. There are a lot of bored people out there, but the truth is you never have to be bored, ever. Just open your eyes, and look at things with wonder as if you are seeing them for the very first time. At the very least, I thought I could help people open their eyes to the

for Trolls," or even, "I Survived the Opening of the Reverend Jen's Lower East Side Troll Museum." T-shirts were flying off the shelves at the Troll Museum's opening, (which went head-to-head with the Damien Hirst opening at Gagosian Gallery) along with Troll Museum fly-swatters, ashtrays, plaques, bumper stickers (which read, "I Brake For Trolls"), Reverend Jen Trolls and picture frames wherein you can commemorate your visit.

On your way out, don't forget to slip some cash into the donation box! Like the Met, we offer a suggested donation. However, because we are just getting started, our price is a bit higher than theirs. ($2,990 higher to be exact.)

The Troll Museum opening was a celebutante-filled extravaganza, which took place on September 23rd, 2000 from noon till 8:00 pm. Budweiser was served, and a tuxedo-clad waiter made his way through the crowd, serving up Marshmallow peeps and cheese as Led Zeppelin blasted out of the stereo, and guests mingled. At the evening's crescendo, I performed a "ribbon cutting" ceremony, which was unfortunately aborted when the ribbon unceremoniously fell off the wall. Following the opening, I held the Troll Museum's first benefit dinner this past July, at Collective Unconscious. The benefit dinner was an evening of page-six-worthy decadence. Up-and-coming power-pop quartet, The Star Spangles played and famed actress / comedian Janeane Garofalo attended, as did punk icon / author, Legs McNeil! Rumor has it that the Hilton sisters even dropped by! But, enough of my name-dropping. (Someone's going to trip all over all the names I dropped!) The dinner featured conceptual ice sculptures (bags of ice in a kiddie pool) as well as a striking troll-shaped cake!

The dinner was necessary because the Troll Museum is not supported by government or private grants. The Troll Museum is in fact supported entirely by me, and I work part-time as a cashier!

Over the course of the past year and a half, it has been my

LES Tenement Museum.) If you make it up the arduous six-flights, you will be greeted by me or by one of the museum's other troll experts / docents, who will open the door for you, thus revealing the most colorful array of trolls you've ever seen in you life! (OK, there are people who have more extensive and valuable collections than I do, but it is not my intention to "show off." I simply want to share with the world what I deem to be the magical qualities of the one of the most incredible toys on Earth.)

The docent will then take your jacket and offer you a Budweiser, a Pop Tart or cheese, and will begin your hour-long tour, where you will learn more about trolls than you ever expected to know in one lifetime. You will see a two-headed troll (the "Mona Lisa" of our museum) which is encased in an alarmed, plexiglass cube, a sight which is made all the more phenomenal by the fact that said troll sports a cowboy outfit and a tiny gun! You will see a pregnant troll, a hippy troll, a punk-rock troll, a troll who had its face burned off by a blow torch, troll puppets, troll "lace huggers," naked trolls, clothed trolls, big trolls, small trolls, an African-American Troll, a robot-troll, and many, many others. You'll see "Reverend Jen's Homemade Troll Shanty," which features two trolls "doing it" in a bed, which is littered in tiny cans of Budweiser. (Put that in your pipe and smoke it, MOMA!) You will bear witness to "Trollies" and "Troll," two troll-related videos, which a skilled docent will allow you to view, and you will also be treated to the sounds of "The Wishnik Family Album" that was made in the 1960s, and which features troll's singing such hits as "London Bridge" and "Ring around the Rosy."

Finally, when you are ready to leave, you can peruse the fabulous gift items at the souvenir stand. We've got colorful, beaded t-shirts that sport catchy slogans like "Out of Con-TROLL at Reverend Jen's Lower East Side Troll Museum," "I went to Reverend Jen's Lower East Side Troll Museum and All I Got Was this Lousy T-Shirt and a Whole New Appreciation

Chapter Eight
Reverend Jen's Lower East Side Troll Museum

It has been called the "eighth wonder of the world." (By one person). It has been called "a Disneyland for Intellectuals." It has been called many things, but one thing is certain—it is America's only Troll Museum. Despite the fact that Mount Horeb, Wisconsin refers to itself as "the Troll Capital of America." The truth of the matter is that the Lower East Side is the actual troll capital of America. While Mount Horeb does have giant statues of trolls along its highways and byways, many of these trolls are reminiscent of Norwegian trolls, and they do not properly pay homage to the kitsch American troll, which rose to fame during the flower power era. Not to mention, if Mount Horeb were really the troll capital of America, don't you think they'd have a Troll Museum for crying out loud? The LES, on the other hand, has its very own Troll Museum, which was opened by myself during the fall of 2000. the LES Museum focuses on American Trolls, which were produced from 1963 till the present day. (We also have an International shelf, which displays trolls from Norway, Mexico and Denmark, where viewers can compare and contrast American trolls to trolls of other countries.) *(Please Note: Despite the fact that I refer to certain trolls as "American" the prototype for many of these trolls was carved by Thomas Dam in Denmark.)*

The Troll Museum is located in the living room of my dilapidated six-floor walk-up tenement apartment, which is located just a block away from the LES's other museum. (The

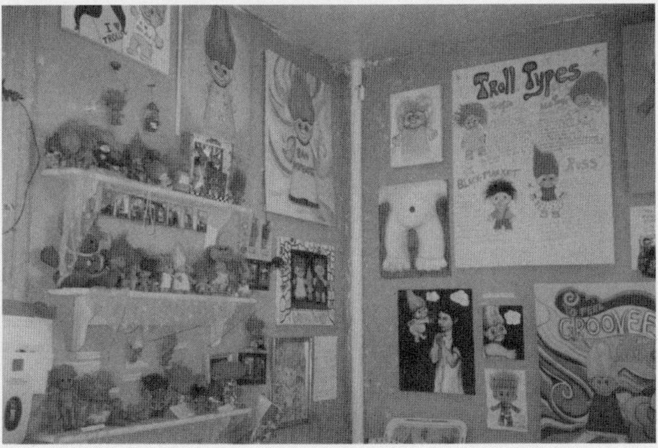
Troll Types

gunning two Budweiser's, I welcomed him to my museum. We have been dating ever since.

Talk to people! No one will know what a fascinating creature you are until you open your mouth and let your brilliance flow from your tongue!

Burn candles. OK, so I don't really believe in all that new age shit, but I am also not willing to rule anything out. Wiccan friends have told me that red candles will bring you passionate love. (I have one burning right now!)

Go to Kinkos late on a Saturday night. Even if you have nothing to copy, find something to copy. A lot of lonely folks call Kinkos home on Saturday nights.

Come to think of it, I really don't know much about finding love on the LES. I know where to find pizza and beer, but not love. If my suggestions fail you, I can only recommend heading over to Toys in Babeland or the Essex Street porn and video store, and picking up some pornography.

have witnessed the blossoming of several long-term and several not-so-long-term relationships, and feel it is my duty to share some tips on how to meet chicks or dudes on the LES.

Buy them a drink. We all know that alcohol is the greatest social lubricant in the world. What we often overlook is that it also the greatest catalyst to romance that the world has ever known. And, with the rising prices of drinks in area bars, your love interest will be especially grateful if you toss them a freebie. (Do not buy them several drinks. You are not offering to be their sugar-parent, just their love interest, and you don't want to send the wrong message.)

Listen. the LES is filled with egomaniacs. Play into their megalomania by pretending that they are the most fascinating creature you've ever spoken to.

Be wary! Today's one-night stand is tomorrow's stalker. (Didn't we learn anything from *Fatal Attraction*?)

Go to open mikes. Having been an open mike host for the past six years, I can tell you that open mikes attract incredibly creative, sexually adventurous people who also suffer from low self-esteem, and who are waiting for someone like you to make them feel beautiful. (This is not a cheap plug for my open mike.) One couple who met at my open mike even got married, and several people who I didn't think would ever get laid in their lives, found true love at my open mike.

Open a Museum. When I opened a Troll Museum (to be covered in the next chapter) in my apartment a couple of years ago, it was not with the intention of finding a boyfriend. However, I was delighted when an art star that I'd had a fleeting crush on for years, e-mailed me asking if he could visit my museum. After cleaning my museum for ten hours and shot-

Chapter Seven
Love Connections

Many of the bars and hangouts on the LES don't seem to fall into the "meat-market" variety. However, this does not mean that bars on the LES aren't filled with hipsters who are looking to enjoy an evening or two of ravenous lovemaking or perhaps even an emotion-draining relationship. And, it certainly doesn't mean that the LES isn't filled with sluts. Quite the contrary! There are a lot of slutty, open minded, bisexual, absurdly attractive people wandering the area south of Houston Street looking for companionship.

There are plenty of "love connections" being made all around the LES. Chances are, if you go out on the LES, you will not be hit on by any dude openly displaying several gold chains in a field of chest hair. I have been drinking in other neighborhoods, and trust me, dudes elsewhere are sleazier, and more apt to harass a woman alone, who simply wants to drown the reality of her failing career as an artist in booze. (However, ladies, be warned—just because a dude has long hair or looks hip, does not mean that he is not a misogynist. The next time you are attracted to a dude with long hair, ask yourself, "Would I like this person if they were wearing a Yankees cap and khakis?") Also, ladies: If you are looking to meet a man who has a job, look elsewhere. And, dudes: If you are looking to meet a woman who is interested in procreating and contributing to the continuation of your lineage, look elsewhere. However, if you are looking for a fun-loving, functioning alcoholic, the LES bar / theater scene is a great place to meet that special someone.

While I am certainly no expert on finding romance, I

wine by saying, "This is the blood of Christ, therefore it's divine." Instead of just saying, "This wine is divine." That's just not good enough. But, I think if the "blood of Christ" had been something gross like Metamucil, communion would've never taken off.

"Sal"

of the Gods elsewhere. None of the places we called were open, so we were actually forced to leave the building. We hit the streets like wild, ravenous dogs. Everything was closed, but off in the distance I spotted a run-down little restaurant called "The Donut King."

Let me tell you something about The Donut King. I don't know what city, state or province he rules, but I know that I never want to go there. Let me tell you something else about The Donut King. You can get donuts there, but don't EVER get pizza there, ever.

I liken my experience at Donut King to a bad cotton swab experience. Cleaning one's ears is pleasurable, especially if one uses brand-name "Q-tips" but imagine using sharp cotton swabs that cause your ears to bleed profusely, and you have some idea of what Donut King pizza was like.

Now, imagine a bulky man in a dirty apron, with snot dripping out of his nose, down his chin, serving the most heinous looking slice you've ever seen, made all the more heinous by the cruel, fluorescent lights, which only serve to highlight its greasiness. "How bad can it be?" I shrugged. After all, it was pizza. When I first attempted to lift the slice to my lips, it fell apart because it was so greasy. This didn't even stop me though. I picked at it, and had three or four more bites before finally calling it quits. Julia also had a couple bites, and later threw up.

While this was a harrowing experience, we realized the smart thing to do, was to get right back on the wagon, go out and have a good slice. Once again, I love pizza. I think it's even safe to say that pizza is my favorite food. In fact, if Catholicism had offered a communion wherein pizza was the body of Christ, and Budweiser was the blood of Christ, I would probably be a Catholic today. Of course, wine (the blood of Christ) is good, but I think it's manipulative on the part of the Catholic Church to claim that wine is something else, and that's why it's good. Like they have to justify drinking

pizza places have rollinis, but I can assure you they don't make 'em like Sal makes 'em.

As I mentioned before, there are several other pizza places downtown, and one of my fave raves above Houston Street is Two Boots on Avenue A and Third Street. The pizza there is different, spicy almost, but it sure is tasty! At Two Boots, you can get all kinds of criz-az-y toppings on your slice, including crawfish and shrimp! Children (under 12) can even get a "pizza face" personal pizza, which I'm assuming has a face on it made out of food products. Of course, I'll never know due to the ageist nature of Two Boots pizza face policy. Attached to Two Boots, there is a video store and a theater.

Another good pizza place on the LES is "Joe's Pizza" on Essex Street. Just because Sal's is the premiere pizza spot on the LES, doesn't mean there aren't others, which you might wanna dine at in case Sal's isn't open. (God forbid!) There is even a kosher pizza place on Grand Street, just slightly east of Essex. One important rule of thumb regarding pizza consumption is: Never get a slice at a food establishment that specializes in another sort of food. In other words, ONLY GET YOUR PIZZA AT A PIZZA PLACE. I have had only one bad pizza experience in my lifetime, and it happened while I was living at The Parkside, and it was bad enough, that it almost turned me off of pizza forever.

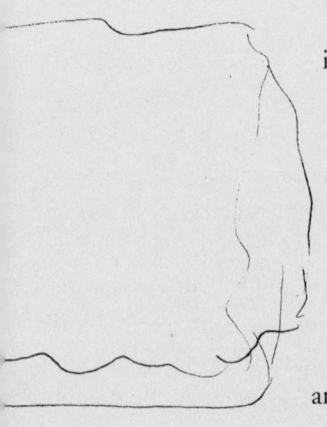

I had been rendering an incredibly anal retentive drawing for class, and I hadn't slept in days. My stomach was a symphony of hunger pangs, all crying out for pizza. Unfortunately, it was 4 am, and Imperial (a pizza place on 34th Street, which I was fond of whilst living in the Gramercy Park area) closed at 2, so Julia and I were forced to seek our food

mouth without having to wait for it to cool. However, I never eat a slice without first removing excess grease. (And, Rosario's is particularly greasy.) Grease removal can be performed in one of two ways. The first way, which is more theatrical and fun, is to take your slice out to the sidewalk, fold it over, and shake it out, in the direction of the ground, allowing the grease to drip off the slice and onto the sidewalk. (Be careful if you're wearing a nice dress or suit, that there are no gale force winds blowing, which might redirect the grease in your direction.) The second, more common method of grease removal is to take a stack of napkins and simply pat the slice until all of the grease has been absorbed. Once you no longer see a shiny inch of grease on your slice, it is ready to eat!

There are many varieties of slices at Sal's. There is even a cheese-less slice for vegans, or anyone who's watching their figure. (Helpful hint: Do not eat the cheese-less slice before a big date as it is loaded in garlic. If you've been dating someone for a while and don't think they'll give a shit about your heinous garlic breath, then by all means, go for it!) One thing that Rosario's has, which has brought them a great deal of acclaim, is the famed rollini. This specialty is cheap—only two bucks, and it's an amazing alternative to pizza if you're feeling a little pizza-weary. It is a somewhat phallic roll of dough, which is stuffed with a variety of tasty fillings. There is the ever popular, chicken and cheese, the cheese and spinach and the pepperoni and cheese, not to mention others. I know other

only time I ever heard him curse.

A couple months later, a generic-looking "Ray's Famous Pizza" was erected in the lot that was previously Sal's, and Sal began working as a pizza man at a little pizza place across the street from K-mart on 34th Street, far away from the magical land of the Lower East Side. Any local who had a shred of decency refused to eat at Ray's, but there were several (including Roommate #2) who did eat there, a fact which horrified me, seeing as how there are so many pizza places in this city, which are not directly responsible for displacing Sal, and which would have been decent alternatives. I personally found an alternative in "New Sicas" a decent pizza place on Rivington and Allen. My friend, J-Boy, and I spent hours plotting how we would unleash bags of crickets at Ray's. We often used to walk in, take a handful of menus, and throw them out, or we would write "crap" on them and put them back. Unfortunately, the LES is mobbed with tourists, who don't know the sordid history of Ray's hostile takeover, and so they naively wander into Ray's.

Finally, much to the joy of the neighborhood, Rosario's opened back up in 2000 at its new location at Stanton and Orchard. Business there is booming, and Sal is back and better than ever. He recently showed me how he has planted mint plants in the sad little patches of grass on Stanton. When you brush your hand against them, and then hold your hand to your nose and inhale, you can smell the scent of mint!

Now that Rosario's is back, you know where to go in order to avoid feeling like shit the next day. But, what to get there?

I have always been an advocate of the plain slice. The union of cheese, dough and sauce is perfection. The only reason to ever get toppings is to shake things up ever so slightly, or to occasionally eat a vegetable. When I do order a plain slice there, I am usually so excited to eat my slice that I have to say, "not too hot please," so that I can stuff the slice into my

referred to as "Sal's" a nickname it gets from Sal Rosario, the jovial "pizza man" who works there. (Not to be confused with Sal's on Avenue A, which is actually named "Sal's".)

Rosario's gets its name from the Rosario family who first opened their establishment on Houston Street, between Orchard and Ludlow, in the mid-1960's. I believe (although this is based only on what I've heard) that Sal came here from Sicily in the '60s and began at that time, to work for a relative who owned the original Houston Street Rosario's. I first began eating at Sal's in 1995, and I developed camaraderie with Sal, who I quickly noticed develops camaraderie with everyone. Locals don't go to Sal's for the pizza, albeit good, they go there for the love. Sal, the most tireless pizza man in the Western hemisphere, is there practically every damn day until after four in the morning, and he's always smiling, even when he is serving up slices to useless, drunk frat-boys.

Rosario's has seen its share of rough times over the years, but it has survived thanks to Sal's dedication to coating the walls of the stomachs of the masses with grease. The gentrification of the LES brought greedy business owners below Houston Street, who were hungry to make a buck, even at the expense of small businesses. Unfortunately, one of those small businesses turned out to be Rosario's. When a "Ray's Famous Pizza" owner bought the block of property where Rosario's lay, and Rosario's lease subsequently ran out, Rosario's got the boot. This brought anger and resentment from area residents, many of whom ate three meals a day at Sal's. People protested. The Times wrote an article. It was a travesty. Sal, who had hand-delivered pizza to the Neo-Futurists every Friday night at their show, who always told me I looked beautiful, even when I came in at three in the morning with my false eyelashes falling off and my hair in disarray, and who most importantly developed the "rollini" now stood with tears in his eyes, serving up slices like a podling who had had its life sucked out by the venomous Skeksis. "Bastards," he said quietly. It was the

Chapter Six
Pizza

Part of drinking responsibly means coating the walls of your stomach with grease so that you don't feel too hung over the next day. I have found that nothing works better at preventing hangovers than pizza.

I am not sure exactly what happens inside my stomach when I eat pizza after a night of heavy drinking, but I think that the pizza is like a Pac-Man, which gobbles up the excess beer floating around inside me. I don't know if there have been any scientific studies on this amazing process, but after I win Publisher's Clearing House, I am going to open up a Center for the Study of Pizza on Drunks, where my friends will be the guinea pigs, who sit around drinking all day, and then scientists will come around with clipboards and slices of pizza, and take notes as my friends eat the pizza. Right now, I think the theory that the pizza "coating the walls of the stomach with grease" theory is more of an urban myth than fact.

What I do know, is that pizza works, and I am grateful, whenever I am boozing, and a friend turns to me, and with shaman-like wisdom, suggests we get a slice, thus sparing me the agony of a hangover.

With this in mind, you will want to know where to get the best pizza after an evening of bar-hopping, so that you too, can avoid the travails of being hungover.

There are many pizza places on the LES, but there really is only one pizza place that matters, and that pizza place is Rosario's on the Northwest corner of Stanton and Orchard. If one were to liken pizza places to discos of the 1970's, Rosario's would be Studio 54. In the local vernacular, Rosario's is often

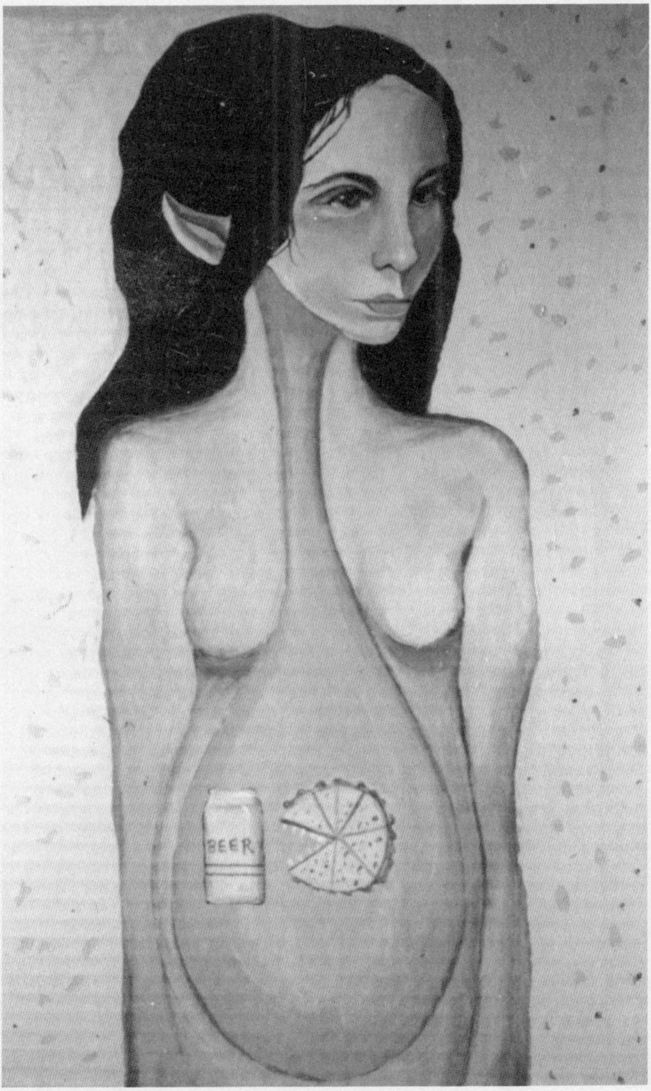
BEER

Drugs are illegal, but beer is legal!

subsequent poverty, I could still delude myself with alcohol.

I guess that about wraps up our chapter on drinking, bars, Budweiser and art openings. Have fun, and remember to always drink responsibly. This will take us directly into our next chapter on pizza.

---

8. Even though I am horrible at math, I recently tried to estimate how much beer was consumed during the first six years of the Anti-Slam. If there are 52 weeks in the year, (I don't know if that's right) that would mean there are 52 Wednesdays in a year. And, if there are roughly between 60 and 70 people at each Anti-Slam, I would guess about 52 of those people drink Budweiser each week (a light estimate). Let's assume each of those 52 has three beers (again, a very low estimate). That's 155 Budweisers! Multiply that by 52 weeks and you've got 7,060 Budweisers! Multiply that by six years, and you've got 42,360 Budweisers. Multiply that by 12 ounces and you've got 508,320 fluid ounces of Budweiser consumed at the Anti-Slam!!!

Another fave of mine is Deitch Projects. I recently attended an opening at Deitch Projects, which is also located downtown, which was sponsored by "Magic Hat" beer, a little known, yet very tasty, beer. Not only that, they had lady wrestling in the back room, and free hair cuts in the side room (where the hairdresser, Christian, tied the people who were getting the hair cuts to a chair, and had some sort of amplified instrument attached to his scissors, so that the act of hairdressing became musical. Not to mention, he gave a damn good haircut.)

In Chelsea, it's really hit or miss. Stefan Stux had hard booze the last time I was there. But, I got there late, and they had run out of mixers, so I was forced to hold my nose and drink it straight like a true alcoholic. I was also recently at a party at American Fine Arts where there were trash cans full of beer! (However, this was at a party. Some of their openings are alcohol-free, while still others have loads of booze, but it is definitely one gallery where the staff will not frown upon you walking in with a giant beer.) At Patterson Beckwith's opening there recently, Patterson provided opening attendees with adorable 8 oz. Buds and tons of cheese and crackers!

When I was a fledgling art star, my instructors at SVA forced me to go to art galleries every week, so that I could familiarize myself with contemporary art. Perhaps, what they should have been teaching me was what galleries served booze so that after my graduation and

your ass off, and you can barely move your wrists, never mind hand the wine and cheese-chasers yet another glass of chardonnay, which they will sip whilst resting one shoe against the wall, which you painted only yesterday, and, which will be covered in unsightly scuff marks by 9 p.m.

If you do go to openings, be sure you are nice to the gallery workers. (Unless they work at one of the more "uppity" galleries, and they are rude to you, in which case, let your inner Sweathog take over.)

"How do I know which galleries are generous with the booze, Reverend Jen?" you ask. Good question. My first word of advice is practice. Go to many openings, until you find the galleries that are right for you.

However, I can tell you of a few galleries where you are pretty much guaranteed a little booze. (Please remember, these recommendations are only based only on my first hand experiences. They are not set in stone. A gallery that serves fine wine one day could go broke the next, and the first thing to go would be the opening booze.)

First on my list of galleries would have to be Leo Koenig at Broadway. This gallery is "special" because it is located conveniently downtown and because Leo provides the gallery-goers with a keg. This unpretentious, generous move has endeared me to this gallery for life. And, if you do happen to get there too late to enjoy the keg, there is a deli next door that sells 24 oz. Buds.

Chapter Five, Part D.
(Art Openings)

When you live on the LES, there are maybe only three reasons to ever leave your neighborhood, and one of them is art openings. For many young artists, openings offer an opportunity to schmooze with art dealers and critics, in an attempt to obtain shows or recognition. For many young alcoholics, openings offer an opportunity to drink as much free wine as possible between the hours of 6 and 8.

However, I urge you: DO NOT GET YOUR HOPES UP! It is 2002, not 1985. Gone are the days of excessive wine, cheese and glamour. At most art openings these days, most of the artists and dealers look like they just stepped out of a Gap ad and most of the openings have about as much wine as an Alcoholic's Anonymous Christmas Party. I have even noticed a disturbing trend, especially at several Williamsburg galleries, where the gallery actually sells wine and beer. In this instance, I say, just get a liquor license and become a bar! Yet, there are still some galleries who carry the torch, who continue to provide the masses with wine and beer in the face of art market instability, and these are the galleries whose openings I go to.

Often, you'll hear gallery workers and gallerists complain that people only come to their openings for wine. OF COURSE! No one has ever gone to art openings for the art. They are either there to schmooze, or they are there to drink, but they are definitely not there to look at the art. If they were interested in actually seeing the art, they would go to the gallery at a time when there aren't seventy people standing in front of each piece.

However, having worked in a gallery, I have witnessed first hand how utterly grotesque the rush to get to the free wine and beer can be. Say you are a gallery worker. It is opening day. Chances are you have been Xeroxing and installing

such an unusual looking beer! Once the initial hilarity wore off, I fell in love with the regal king of cans. If you walk into an art opening clutching a 40-ounce, people will think you are posturing and trying to look tough, but if you walk into that same opening with a 24-ouncer, people will think only one thing—that you love Budweiser enough to drink it out of a can that NASA can see from telescopes on the moon. No one looks cool drinking a 24, but other Bud drinkers will respect the fact that you've opted for the two-beers-in-one can. This is the flashiest Bud of all, and for all you guys and gals who are watching your waistlines, it comes in light variety as well!

(Best place to buy 24-ounce cans: Stop One bodega, located at 172 Allen Street, where there is always a hefty supply located in the upper right hand corner of the cooler.)

The 40-ounce bottle: If you're drinking a forty, you're probably not kidding around. You want to get drunk. After all, it's three and a half beers in one! Not to mention, if you don't want your arms to get tired, you'd best drink it quick, which means you'll only be drunker! This is the heavy weight champ, the Big Kahuna, the King Kong of cans. Drink it with caution.

in a dozen, cans in a 12-pack, hours in a clock, and number of ounces in the glorious twelve ounce can. This is the ultimate classic. If one were to liken Budweiser to perfume, this would be Chanel No. 5. You really can't go wrong here. It's like a favorite pair of jeans that you haven't washed in two weeks, so they slide on nice and easy. The ultimate symbol of the abolition of prohibition, it comes in the light, ice and regular varieties. The 12-ounce is the corner stone of American civilization.

The 12-ounce Bud bottle: Bottles are always a bit pricier than cans, and I think it's because they are supposed to stay cold longer. For this reason, they are a bit considered a bit "classier" than the can, by the nouveau riche, who have not yet learned to accept the simplistic beauty of the 12-ounce can. This also comes in light, ice and regular.

The 16-ounce can, or tall boy: This one is extremely popular on the Lower East Side. I'd even venture to say that it has replaced the 12-ounce as the Bud of choice. But what can you expect from Americans? After all, America invented the Super-Sized value meal and the Eldorado Cadillac. It's only 4-ounces bigger than the standard 12-ounce, so you almost feel like you're drinking a regular Bud, but within moments of finishing just two of these bad boys, you should start to note a shift in your ability to perceive reality!

The 16-ounce bottle: This is perhaps the subtlest of all Bud varieties. If one were to liken different types of Bud to various artists, the 16-ounce bottle would most certainly be Robert Ryman. It's not flashy, and it's only for the true aficionado.

The 22-ounce bottle: This is a good pre-performance beverage from any stage performer who suffers from occasional stage fright. It doesn't quite equal two beers, and it packs more of a love tap than a punch, so that, upon imbibing one, you won't forget your lines, you will deliver them with ease.

The 24-ounce can: The first time I saw a 24, I must've laughed for 20 minutes. Never before in my life had I seen

simple: A 40 is too heavy. Who wants to lift weights and drink beer? Not me! Not to mention, a 40 will get warm if it's not consumed quickly enough."

I say this, not to speak ill of the 40, but to praise the 24. Variety is good, from the tiniest 8-ounce to the looming 40. And, if you do choose to drink the King of Beers, you should be well schooled in the many varieties of Bud, which are available to the public, so that when you visit your local bodega or grocery store, you are able to make an informed decision. Below, I have prepared a list of the different types of Budweiser that you may want to familiarize yourself with, so that you will feel comfortable upon making your beer selection at one of the many neighborhood bodegas. (Please Note: I do not work for Budweiser, and I am only an expert in so far as I have observed Budweiser closely. There may in fact be more types of Budweiser than I have listed here!)

The 7-ounce pony: They don't sell these on the Lower East Side. I have really only seen these little waifs at weddings and at liquor stores, 7-11's and grocery stores in Ocean City, Maryland.

The 8-ounce: This is the "elf" of beers. It sure is cute! And, in keeping with its elfin nature, it mischievously comes in an 8-pack! Like the 24-ounce it presents onlookers with a surreal, and ultimately confusing image—a can so small, it makes tiny hands look big, and big hands look gigantic!

The 10-ounce Bud Light: This is a weird one. The first time I saw it, thought I was hallucinating! The strange thing about the ten-ounce is that it only seems to come in the "light variety." But, at two for a dollar, who cares? These are hard to find. However, they always have them at the bodega on Stanton, between Ludlow and Orchard that smells like cat-pee, and has meat hanging in the window.

The 12-ounce Bud can: Twelve: The number of apostles in the Bible, Astrological signs in the Zodiac, animals in the Chinese calendar, months in a year, inches in a ruler, cookies

Fun Activity:
Get your friends together, and call 1-800-DIAL-BUD.
Ask the Budweiser representative how many
different sizes of Budweiser there are.
If they slip up, be sure to let them know.

they often prefer TV movies to club bathrooms.

However, Budweiser is not only the beverage of choice for quiet get-togethers amongst friends. It is also the beverage of choice for off-off-off Broadway audiences and performers alike. Many of my stage props have even been built out of Bud cans!

For the past six years, on Wednesday nights, I have hosted *Reverend Jen's Anti-Slam*, an anything-goes open mike (See Chapter Eight on open mikes), where massive quantities of Budweiser are consumed each week.[8] In fact, when art stars would visit the local bodega, in order to purchase Budweiser before the show, the proprietors of said bodega, would assume that this meant the person purchasing their Bud was on their way to a theater, and they would say, "Enjoy the Show!" (Unfortunately Vega Baja was a victim of gentrification. It shut down in '98.) After every show I toss hundreds of empty Budweiser cans into the recycling bin, and the not too complex conclusion I have drawn from this after-show ritual is that art stars truly love Budweiser, specifically, giant 24-ounce cans of Bud. Perhaps it is the surreal nature of the 24-ounce can, or perhaps it is the economical value, but one thing is certain. It is very popular.

In my first book, *Sex Symbol for the Insane*, I discuss the 24-ounce at great length, and I will not repeat that essay here. (Just a taste! You gotta buy my other book if you want the two-course meal! And, don't forget to pick up the *Cliff Notes* while you're at it!) Nevertheless, I would like to share with you some of the more spectacular qualities of the 24-ounce in an abbreviated form.

For starters, the 24 is the prefect size. It's two beers in one, so you only need one bottle. (Sort of like a shampoo plus conditioner so you only need one bottle!) I'd even venture to say that it's the greatest thing since sliced bread. In fact, sliced bread isn't even as good because if a slice of bread isn't sliced, you can just slice it! Why not just drink a 40?" you ask. It's

Sunday" law. Separation of Church and State—Hello?!!!)

Mayoral hopeful (or whatever the Hell he was), Christopher X. Brodeur has offered a course of action that many citizens can adopt in order to deactivate these silly laws. His suggestion is that beer-lovers pour their beers into soda cans, and soda lovers pour their soda into beer cans. The first time a cop stops a pedestrian for drinking out of a Bud can in order to give them a ticket, and said pedestrian proves that they are not in fact drinking beer, but rather, Dr. Pepper, that cop is going to feel mighty silly, and mighty hesitant when it comes to stopping others for similar offenses. Brodeur has even suggested marketing a brand of beer called "Cloak-a-Cola."

But I digress. I'd also like to add, that while I feel Giuliani did succeed in squashing nightlife, Downtown is still very much alive. (I suppose I am only saying this because I never got to experience Downtown while it was alive.) I'd even venture to say that the art Downtown has gotten better. (Mainly, because there is no longer the draw of edgy nightclubs to distract artists from their work. There is also no money for artists. Artists from previous generations complained because they had their grants taken away. I graduated art school with the knowledge that I would probably never receive a grant for anything.) I graduated from art school in 1994. There had already been a backlash against political art. Everyone wanted to be Mathew Barney. It was a very sad time. The art world was financially in shambles, and nightlife had become "safe" and lame as shit.

On a personal level, I feel this is a good thing. Had there been great clubs, plentiful drugs and lots of dough in town at that time, I probably would not be working on this book at this moment, but I would probably be sitting in an uncomfortable chair at an NA meeting nervously clutching a cigarette, and drinking coffee.

But, once again, I am sidetracked. Downtown is alive and well, only its inhabitants prefer Budweiser to cocaine, and

ing Budweiser with these very people, until Giuliani began cracking down on this too. (And, actually, it was not just Giuliani. Puritanism, which all too often rears its ugly head in attempts to curb public drunkenness, has taken hold of many other cities as well. I once got a ticket for drinking a 40 of King Cobra with some friends in a Hoboken playground in 1993. Fortunately, the cops wrote the date for when I had to appear in court on the ticket, and when I examined it next to a calendar, I realized that they had accidentally scheduled my court date for a Sunday! Lucky me!) Fortunately, I have heard that if the cop fails to write down what type of beer it is you are drinking, your ticket will be nullified, and the charges will be dropped. (I don't know if this is true, but I do know that you can do as I have done, and get a childish looking thermos [mine is Teletubbies] in which to carry your beer, in order to save yourself from ever having to go through the legal system.)

Currently, the crackdown on drinking Budweiser on the sidewalks of New York is extremely heavy, and I would advise never drinking beer directly out of its original container on NYC streets and sidewalks, EVEN IF IT'S IN A PAPER BAG!

The extremity with which NYC wields punishment upon those who transgress the public drinking laws is not to be believed. My friend, Larry, recently told of a sight he witnessed upon his return from the financial district, on September 11th, 2001. A man, covered in soot and debris, walked up Broadway, clutching a beer. A police officer asked him to pour out his beer. He adamantly refused. Nothing the policeman said could have made this gentleman, who probably was an extremely gentle man who only wanted to numb himself at that moment, could have made him throw out his beer, so that two armed police officers TACKLED the poor man to the ground and wrestled the beer out of his hands.

I say the crackdown on public drinking has gone too far. I say ALL laws pertaining to drinking have gone too far. (I won't even attempt to get into the "no liquor before noon on

Budweiser is cheap. It is good. And, it contains alcohol. Therefore, artists drink it.

Attempting to become a successful artist is a painful process that is more often than not, plagued by desperation, poverty, despair and rejection. If it weren't for Budweiser, many of us would sober up, and realize that we are delusional for expecting any level of artistic recognition. Budweiser feeds our delusions and makes life bearable.

Recently, my friend, Faceboy, and I were asked to entertain a seventeen-year old girl named Danielle, who was visiting New York for the weekend. She wanted to see "New York nightlife." What Danielle saw was Faceboy and I sitting in his room with an eighteen-pack of Budweiser, watching *C'mon Get Happy*, the NBC *Partridge Family Story*, TWICE IN A ROW! We were forced to explain to Danielle that our former Mayor had succeeded in destroying NY nightlife, so that we were forced to behave in this reclusive manner.

However, this is only partly true. While Giuliani did succeed in closing down topless joints and padlocking and harassing several bars, we also like television movies and sitting in our rooms. It is an unfortunate fact that most of the people who live in New York are horrible. (Being a misanthrope, I believe that most people who live in most places are horrible. But, please note: I did not say, "Most people are evil." I still think people are decent, I just find them unbearable.) However, New York contains a portion of people who are not only not horrible, they are people who were brave enough to come to New York in order to fulfill their dreams, and those are the people I love, the people I want to sit in rooms with, watching TV Movies and drinking Budweiser.

I also used to greatly enjoy sitting on the stoops of schools and buildings throughout the city, drink-

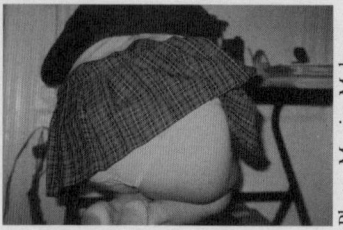

Photo: Monica Mohan

Chapter Five, Part C.
(Budweiser)

As I mentioned in the conclusion of Part B., many area bars have become unaffordable and far too crowded, and this is where Budweiser begins to play a major role in the lives of many LES residents and visitors. In Part C., we will discuss the qualities that Budweiser possesses, which make it the King of Beers.

For starters, Budweiser is the official drink of the Lower East Side.

You can find it in every bodega south of Houston Street, and you can find it lovingly cupped in the hands of the Lower East Side's inhabitants.

"But, Reverend Jen," you protest. "I thought only beer-swilling, football-watching rednecks drank Budweiser. Aren't you guys bohemians?"

Yes, we are bohemians, but Budweiser is "The King of Beers" and this means that it appeals to a wider audience than most people realize. There are almost as many varieties of Budweiser as there are types of people who drink it, and this is part of its appeal.

ly visit all of them, without occasionally checking myself into the Betty Ford Clinic, which until this book becomes a best seller, I can't afford.

While there are many delightful bars in this city, I have noticed a decline in both the hospitality and the entertainment value of many of the city's bars. I am not sure if this is due to Giuliani's crack down on nightlife (his enforcement of the cabaret laws, and his general anti-fun sentiment) or to a wide-ranging cheapness that seems to have permeated many New York City bars. These days, you practically have to beg for a buy-back, even after the third drink, and even if you left a good tip, in order to get one! It is very sad time for those of us, who once relied upon the kindness of bartenders in order to keep our livers in a constant state of corrosion.

so far uptown) I had been drinking with my schizophrenic/alcoholic friend, Ayesha, and my boyfriend, Nick. We had been thrown out of Motor City, when Ayesha knocked over a bucket of glue, her limbs being instruments of destruction when under the influence. Upon getting the boot, we found ourselves at Max Fish (Nick's suggestion) where Nick threw a drink in the face of a fat dude, who he claims insulted us. The bartenders politely threw us out, and despite the fact that the last thing we needed was more booze, we traipsed into The Library, looking disheveled and unwanted. While the bartenders at Max Fish refused to serve Ayesha, the bartenders at The Library were more than happy to continue to pour drinks down her throat. Not only that, they bought us a round of shots! When Ayesha wasn't looking, I quickly stole her shot, which was some sort of heinous, banana schnapps concoction, in order to prevent her from plunging further into her abysmal drunkenness, and when I noticed Nick gagging due to the grossness of the banana-flavor, I grabbed his shot and quickly poured it down my throat, an act which received uproarious approval from the other bar-patrons. This brought me to the conclusion that The Library is a great place to hang out, if you want others to encourage and commend your own infantile, drunken behavior. There was absolutely no attitude, no pretentiousness, and no women in tiny high-heels, sipping martinis. It was less rugged and repulsive than Mars Bar, but it still contained a musky odor and rough edge. And, if that's not enough for ya, there's also a movie screen at the back of the bar, where B-Movies are played on a regular basis! I would prefer not to jump to any rash conclusions about a bar that I've only been to a couple of times, but after last night, I believe I can safely give it two drunken thumbs up.

In Conclusion

All this talk about bars is making me thirsty, and quite frankly, with so many bars on the Lower East Side, I can hard-

cocaine under her nose. My entire evening at Chaos consisted of paltry arguments with the staff. For starters, the music that their DJ chose to spin was some sort of '80s music that made my pointed elf ears curl up in fear. When I ascended to the DJ booth in order to suggest something more in the order of Abba Gold, a giant bouncer yelled at me for "trespassing" the DJ booth. Shortly after the hour of free tequila ended, I collected my friends all of whom had reached transcendental states of inebriation, and headed for Luna Lounge.

My Chaos experience did not end there. I was invited to yet another party, one that I had no hand in planning, which was being thrown by In Style magazine at Chaos. I brought along my friends Lard Dog and Monica. Despite the fact that I found Chaos to be hideous, I was not above going back in the name of free champagne. What ensued was drunken buffoonery, but I was horrified when one of the bouncers physically removed the gentle Lard Dog, who had drunkenly wandered in to a private "staff only" room (no doubt where they do the devil's dandruff) whilst looking for a pay phone.

Apart from these two frightful experiences, I have become acquainted with the Chaos clientele because they often accost me, when I am walking down the street, and they are driving down the street in their magenta or turquoise cars, and they slow down to ask me, "Yo, where's Chaos?" And, the sad thing is, I know.

10. The Library (7 Avenue A)

The Library is not a library at all! Rather, it is a mighty fine drinking establishment, which requires no library card or knowledge of the Dewy-Decimal system. It even comes complete with a Chihuahua, who belongs to one of the Library's employees! Although, I was not planning on profiling this little joint, it is fresh in my memory from having gotten drunk there last night. Despite the fact that I rarely go there (it being

disappear. There are also large bowls full of peanuts on each table, and rockin' tunes played at a volume that's not as excessive as Motor City. In fact, I was both thrilled and shocked to hear Donovan playing at the Whiskey Ward late one Saturday night, but realized after they played the same Donovan song over and over, that it was actually 4 a.m., and that this was the bartender's way of trying to get everyone out the door. It had the exact opposite effect on me, a lifelong fan of Donovan!

9. Chaos (225 E. Houston Street)

No bar, club, restaurant or theater deserves a bad review more than this den of sleaze. Chaos is as much a dance club, as it is a bar and this may partially explain why the management feels that it is acceptable to charge 7 dollars for a Budweiser. Many former Goths remember when Chaos used to be The Bank, which catered to vampire teeth-implanted, black wearing young hipsters. Today Chaos, caters to the silicon-implanted Bridge and Tunnel crowd. You might be wondering, how it is that I have actually been to Chaos, in order to report to you on its unbearable suckiness. The truth of the matter is that last year, *SHOUT* magazine, for which I was a columnist, held its Christmas party there. (Jesus Christ's birthday party, to be more accurate.) When we first decided to throw our soiree there, the manager promised us an all night open bar, which is of course, why we agreed to hold the event there. However, only days before the event, said manager, called to inform us that there would be no open bar, but that we would be allotted approximately one hour of free Jose Quervo tequilla. The party started at 8:00 that evening, and by 7:59, a group of my friends had already begun to line up outside of the velvet rope. Once inside, various art stars began pouring tequila into their mouths apace, which apparently disturbed the manager of Chaos, who when she complained about the behavior of our guests to me, had visible mounds of

and who you wouldn't normally expect to see on Ludlow Street. In this sense, it is a refreshing break from the prevalent edginess of the neighborhood. It almost makes me feel like I'm back in Maryland, which is not necessarily a good thing, but is an instant cure for homesickness. (As in one evening of normalness depresses me enough to make me happy to submerge myself in a sea of freaks the following day.)

7. Orchard Bar (200 Orchard Street)

My friend from college, Michael, opened this bar, which means I have to say something nice about it, even though I don't hang out there much anymore. When it first opened, the novelty of knowing that a School of Visual Arts graduate was actually mildly successful enough to open a bar was very exciting. But, as the years have passed, my excitement has dwindled. And, I have to admit that it's not really my scene. On most nights, the music seems to be techno-y stuff. (Due to my complete and total ignorance of all modern music, I refer to anything that doesn't have lyrics as techno.) However, the bartenders are nice and early on weeknights, the place is delightful, dare I say, romantic.

8. Whiskey Ward (121 Essex Street)

This joint is one of the newer bars in town, and it ain't too shabby. Because I only drink beer, I am probably not the best person to be reviewing a bar called "The Whiskey Ward." (I used to drink the hard stuff, but that ended one night after I got completely tanked at the now defunct bar, Siberia, and found myself falling out of a cab onto the sidewalk in front of a group of stunned pedestrians.) The Whiskey Ward has a lot of different types of whiskey at reasonable prices, and they also serve Pabst Blue Ribbon, so it's possible to drink at this establishment without simultaneously watching your paycheck

Even Hercules, the owner's Boston Terrier, looks like it could kick ass and take names. (Don't let his macho visage fool you though. He is well known for traipsing up to customers, and licking them square in the face, lovingly. He also has a whole barrage of hand-made doggie outfits, which make him slightly less edgy.) Speaking of dogs, their presence is not only allowed here, it is encouraged, so this is a great place to go, if you're looking to cheer yourself up by witnessing four-legged friends frolic, but it's a bad place to go, if you're allergic to dog hair.

Motor City has an undeniable "Rock-n-Roll" vibe, and this means there's always a lot of leather (cute boys in leather jackets, not S&M lovers in leather chaps) tattoos, and lots of loud music. Even though I dig much of the music, which is played there I find that the volume at which it is played can be unbearable. I go to bars as much for conversation, as I do for drunken buffoonery, and unless you can read lips, it's not always the best place for conversation. It is, however, the perfect place for bringing a bad date who you have no desire to talk to.

However, Motor City definitely deserves my seal of approval for having given me 75 drink tickets to distribute at a benefit dinner for my Troll Museum.

6. Iggy's Celtic Lounge (132 Ludlow Street)

I can't say I'm a regular at this traditional Irish bar, but I have ventured there once or twice due to the fact that many of the other bars are simply too crowded, and Iggy's is larger than most of the other bars, and therefore, spacious enough to almost always comfortably seat my weary ass. (I am very opposed to standing in bars.) The bartenders at Iggy's are Irish, cute and very susceptible to flattery, so that if you throw enough compliments their way they are sure to throw a shot of booze your way. Iggy's seems to attract a large number of preppy men in starched shirts, who look like they play golf,

"But, Reverend Jen isn't well known." Exactly! The cool thing about "Eating It" is that they deign to feature unknown losers like me alongside professional performers. To quote from a recent *Village Voice* listing; "Performers usually consist of a smattering of intellectuals (college grad, Conan writer types), freaks (Reverend Jen types), and the occasional sketch group." The door cover is somewhere around six dollars. (It used to be five, but inflation drove it up a dollar, and that's why I use the words "somewhere around" because for all I know, by the time you read this, it could cost sixty dollars.)

Also, this is very important: Bring your ID. The bouncer, who looks like Rick James, won't let you in without one.

4. Max Fish (178 Ludlow Street)

Personally, I am not a big fan of this establishment. I know many people who frequent it, and swear that it's a great place, but if you ask me, it's too well lit, and filled with excessive attitude. I once got in a very loud verbal argument with a bouncer at Max Fish, who would not let my friend Monica and I enter the bar, despite the fact that we were both carrying ID. He made fun of our clothes, saying that we dressed like we belonged to the Brady Bunch, and he then suggested that we were sexually repressed and therefore needed to go shopping for dildos. Despite the fact that this was years ago, I have not quite recovered from this experience.

However, Max Fish does occasionally have art shows, with colorful (albeit decorative) work on the walls, which I am content to observe through the windows. They also have pinball, which attracts a great number of art stars. (Mars Bar and Ace Bar also have pinball.)

5. Motor City (127 Ludlow Street)

Two words, which aptly describe this bar are "Bad Ass." It is not a dangerous bar, but many of its customers look dangerous.

tures, and large mirrors, where you can check your reflection to make sure you've still got it together after several rounds. There's plenty of beer on tap, the Mundi martini, and a fruity, orange sangria, which has so much fruit in it, it's like a meal. If you can't find a seat in the front, try the "make-out room" in the back, where I have oft times wandered in on couples playing tonsil hockey, and where a fireplace sizzles in the winter. In the summertime, there's a lovely garden out back, where thanks to large overhead nets, you can chat with your friends, without having bottles hurled at your head by angry neighbors.

The highlight of Barramundi is "Mumma" a devilish, black cat who lurks behind the bar, and gets a kick out of knocking things off the bar, and often playfully scratching drunken customers.

Once after being stood up at Barramundi, I drunkenly wrote Mumma a poem. What follows is an excerpt.

Oh Mumma
Oh Mumma, what prey is it you happen to be stalking?
Your lovely, black fur, speckled with copper cat hair,
If only I could meow, and you could articulate.
If only you were bipedal, and we could dance till sunlight.

3. Luna Lounge (171 Ludlow Street)

I like this bar because I sometimes get free drinks for performing there, and because the owner, Rob, always invites me to their anniversary party, at which I get more free drinks and free pizza from Rosario's. You will like this bar because the bartenders are nice, and because they have good bands play there, often for no cover charge!!! If you are in town on a Monday, you absolutely cannot miss "Eating It" a comedy show, which features many of the city's most well known comedians, like Marc Maron, Dave Cross, Louis C. K., Dave Chapelle, Janneane Garofalo, Wanda Sykes as well as yours truly. You might now be shaking your head sadly, thinking,

moved away from where the enraged man was screaming. Everyone except for Chicken Man, who sat calmly at the bar sipping his cocktail with the finesses of a dandy in turn of the century Paris.

Mars Bar features art on the walls, most of which is hideous and covered in the grime that eventually covers everything there. On occasion Mars Bar puts on art shows where anyone who wants to show their work can bring it to the bar, and it will be hung up, regardless of how poorly it is executed, which doesn't always make for the best shows, but is a far less uppity way of curating a show than the current gallery system.

Speaking of art, the bathrooms at Mars Bar are an ongoing expressionist installation and a scientific experiment in one. I am convinced that if scientists were to take samples off of the toilet seats at Mars Bar, they would find fully developed Anthrax spores and perhaps even alien life forms. My advice: Stay as far away from the toilet seat as humanly possible, and bring your own toilet paper! But, do go. It is both an olfactory and an emotional experience.

2. Barramundi (147 Ludlow Street)

I supported Barramundi for the fiscal years 1996, 97, 98 and 99. At one time it was my favorite bar, and I attended it with the same regularity that Jack, Janet and Chrissy attended the Regal Beagle. In fact, I nicknamed it "The Regal Beagle." And, it would have probably remained my favorite bar, had it not become everyone else in the Western Hemisphere's favorite bar. These days, it is just too goddamn crowded. However, it is still a great bar, with nice, big cozy chairs, and round tables, which I believe are conducive to conversation. So, it is still worth a visit, especially if it is relatively early on a weekday. If it's a weekend, forget it! (Unfortunately, Ludlow Street becomes "Dudelow" Street on weekends.)

The interior of Barramundi is a jumble of surreal sculp-

Chapter Five, Part B.
(Bars)

1. Mars Bar (2nd Avenue and 1st Street, BYTP)

Currently, this is my watering hole of choice, not because it is a "nice" place to drink, but for precisely the opposite reason. It is very un-nice. In fact, it is gross. (It also doesn't hurt that the bartenders there have a habit of serving me free drinks, a fact which could make the foulest bar bearable.) I recently walked by the sewer grates outside of Mars Bar and I noticed that the scent of the bar wafts up to the street, assaulting the noses of unsuspecting pedestrians. Upon venturing inside you will note that the smell only becomes stronger. This will not bother you, when you notice, upon ordering your drink that the drinks are almost half the price of other bars in the city! Not only that, you will be immediately intrigued by the clientele, which includes drunken punk rockers and crazy people, many of whom defy gravity by standing up, when they should have been passed out long ago. Recently, I was sitting at Mars Bar, when I felt something hit my shoe. I thought something had fallen off the bar, but when I looked down, I saw that a man was sleeping on my shoe. Be sure to look for "Chicken Man" a seemingly mild-mannered gray-haired gentleman, who sits at the bar, diligently night after night. Talk to him and you will get one of two reactions—pleasant conversation or incoherent rambling, shouting and screaming his favorite word, "Cocksucker." If you arrive at Mars Bar, but you don't feel like having a drink, don't worry. You Will. I reckon within five minutes of being there you will be driven to drink.

There is always entertainment at this fine establishment. Not long ago, I witnessed a man, who was fighting with a woman, who may or may not have been a hooker, over sixty dollars. The bartender locked the man outside, and the woman inside, but within seconds the man crashed his head through the window in order to finish his argument. Everyone

more cheap bars open.

With this sentiment in mind, I would like to share with you many of my favorite and not-so-favorite spots for drinking on the LES.

about as fast as a monorail at Six Flags. Growing up in Maryland, right outside of D.C., I had to sell my kidneys any time I wanted to get to the Smithsonian. Recently, I made a short trip to L.A., where I discovered that their subway system goes to about all of four stops. Not only is this environmentally irresponsible, it is inhospitable as well. How are you supposed to get anywhere when you're drunk? This lack of a decent subway system seems to be far too conducive either to drunk driving or to staying at home and doing nothing. On the other hand, New York's subway system means that New Yorkers never have to select a designated driver. The New York City subway system is your designated driver.

Personally, I am aware of the fact that I am a horrible driver, and so I took myself off the road several years ago, as a public service to humanity. I am more than happy to live in a town that not only keeps the rest of the world safe from my lack of skill as a driver, but which also allows me to imbibe alcohol whenever the mood strikes.

If New York is the best city in the world for drinking, the Lower East Side is the best neighborhood within the city, in which to drink. The bars are plentiful, the beer is cheap (by New York standards) and the eye-candy is everywhere. (See Chapter Seven—"Love Connections.") In the short time that I have lived here, I have watched the LES blossom into a virtual amusement park of bars. Many long-time residents are unhappy about this, and do their best to see that these drinking establishments are closed down, but happily, drinking and fun prevail. I would like to see more bars open. In fact, I would like to put little, amusement park-style train cars on the sidewalks, which feature bar cars, so that bar-goers can go from bar to bar without ever having to take a break.

I guess this makes me a bit of a hypocrite, since in the last chapter, I stated my negative opinion of the gentrification of the LES, and the opening of bars only serves as a catalyst to gentrification, so allow me to rephrase. I would like to see

Chapter Five
Drinking

It is true that New York City is the city that never sleeps, but it is also the city that never stops drinking. There are two types of New York City residents: drunks, and those currently attending AA. If anyone thinks that they don't fall into either category, it is simply because their potential as a drunk has not been fully explored. Luckily, New York City caters to the exploration of ones own addiction to booze, and no neighborhood caters more hospitably than the Lower East Side. In the city's humble beginnings, gin and rum were added to tap water to assure that it was safe to drink, and most residents opted to drink beer for breakfast instead of coffee. Despite the fact that today, many residents opt for coffee with breakfast, the spirit of excessive drinking is alive and well.

New York City's public transportation system is partly responsible for its denizens' overindulgence in booze. The subways run all night, they go practically everywhere, and they are affordable to boot. Other cities fail to provide their residents with this sort of freedom. In D.C., for instance, The Metro, runs only until 1:00 am, costs and arm and a leg and doesn't go everywhere. In fact, the further outside of the center of D.C. you get, the more money it costs! New York's subways are far more democratic. It's always a buck-fifty, whether you're goin' to the Upper West Side or Yonkers. It simply doesn't matter! (Ok, it really should be cheaper, but I won't get into that here.) One argument you might hear from D.C. Metro-Lovers is, "It's Clean!" So? I'd rather ride a dirty, graffiti-laden, urine-soaked train that's cheap and that gets me to where I need to go, than a sparkling clean, yet pricey train that moves

Photo: Kat Fasano

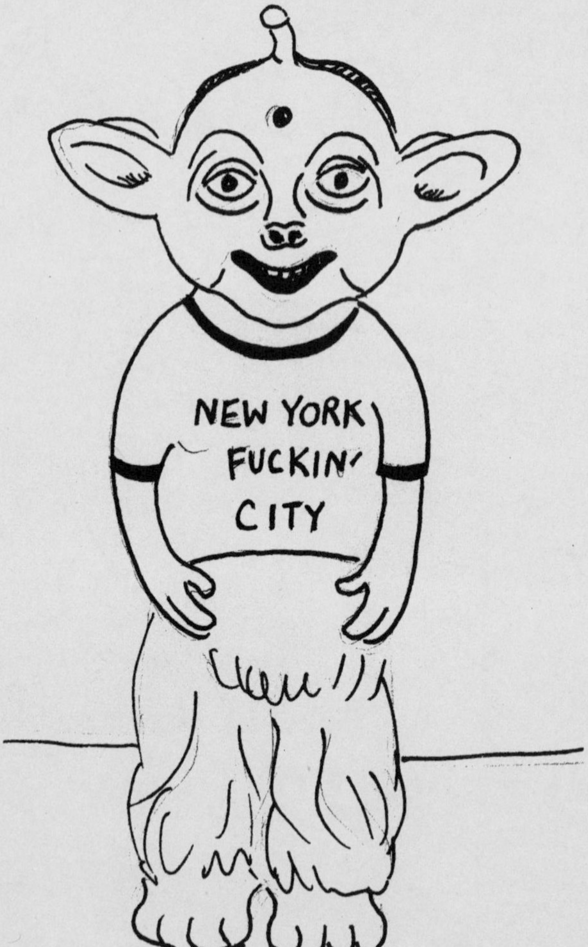
NEW YORK
FUCKIN'
CITY

Realty," is a perfect example of a landlord, who is loath to improve the living conditions of his tenants.

In fact, only a few weeks ago, a crack in my ceiling, which the slumlords had refused to fix, gave way causing a very large portion of my ceiling to cave in just barely missing my head. I am so used to this sort of thing happening that I calmly finished eating my sandwich before calling the slumlords to inform them of my new sunroof. After years of witnessing my landlord's reticence to properly lord over his land, I felt a burning desire to protest, but the question was, "How to protest without being thrown out or maimed?" The answer was simple: PUPPETRY. I performed the first installment of *Les Misrahi,* early one morning directly outside of my landlord's office. In the great tradition of radical puppetry (?), it involves the struggle of a young working-class elf, Jen, to track down the elusive Housing Authority in order to acquire heat and hot water.

For your amusement, I have included the entirety of this epic manuscript at the end of this book.

But enough of my bitterness, let's move onto the fun stuff.

---

7. One word, which continually surfaces in this book is "gentrification" which could be defined as either, the act of making an unprosperous neighborhood prosperous or the act of making a once rockin' neighborhood suck.

about when offered an apartment on the top floor of an ancient building.) When I got to the third floor, I saw a fireman. "It's OK," he said. "You have time."

I got to the bottom, and swooned into his burly arms. He helped Roommate #2 and me descend into the neighboring shoe store where we realized that we were covered in soot.

It wasn't long before the firemen put the fire out and informed us that a crackhead smoking in bed on the 4th floor had been the source of the inferno. Fortunately, the 4th floor was the only one which experienced any significant damage and no one was hurt, so we were able to go home in a few short hours. Unfortunately the firemen had kicked in our door, and we were unable to get back in. Feeling slightly invincible, I climbed out of my next-door neighbor's window, back out onto the fire escape and popped into the window from whence I came.

The most alarming thing about this incident was that there hadn't been a single fire alarm in the hallways or the apartments on the 4th floor. When I called to report this to The Housing Authority, they asked, "Well, are there alarms now?"

"Yes," I said.

"Well, then everything's ok," they answered. I could only imagine how many of my landlord's other buildings still don't have smoke alarms, and how the next time the tenants might not be so lucky. I always knew that landlords don't give two shits about their tenants, but I always thought it was The Housing Authority's duty to at least pretend like they cared. The unfortunate truth is that housing inspectors are like Sesame Street's Snuffleupagus—you almost never see them, and when you do, they disappear.

Living on the Lower East Side is and always has been a battle. Landlords have always been reluctant to make changes, and had the government not interfered in the early part of the 20th century, it is quite possible that many tenements still would have no toilets or showers. My landlord, "Misrahi

roommates. I know someone who once put out an ad in *The Village Voice* when they were looking for a roommate, and her ad said, "no mimes please." Little did she know that later that week, she would receive tons of messages from angry mimes, berating her for her anti-mime sentiment.

If you are willing to put up with lack of privacy, no air-conditioning, sporadic heat, very little hot water, no water-pressure, no closets and excessive noise, this is the neighborhood for you.

Several years ago I was hanging out in my kitchen with Roommate #2 (pre-acting school), shooting the shit, one sunny afternoon. We began to hear sirens, and I said, "Wow. There are a lot of fire engines. That must be some fire."

"Yeah. I can even smell the smoke," Roommate #2 commented.

I looked out the window and I saw several fire engines turn down our street. "It must be really close." I added.

Without thinking, my roommate ran to the front door of our apartment and opened it. (If you think there's a fire in your building do not do this. Touch the door, and if it's hot, get the fuck out.) We were aghast to see a wall of smoke blocking our doorway. We ran to my bedroom, and in an instant that would make MacGyver's head spin, I popped open my window, and jumped out on the fire escape, followed by Roommate #2. A lot of people, who have never been in a fire, discuss what object they would attempt to salvage if they were ever forced to escape from a fire, but the truth is, when the reality of being in a fire hits you, you really couldn't give two shits about your sacred thimble collection. (Of course, if I'd had Rev. Jen Junior at the time, I would have saved her.)

I darted down the fire escape, in my un-laced boot moccasins, which got entangled on the many clotheslines I was forced to contend with. I felt certain that I would either be engulfed in flames or that I would fall through a hole in the deteriorated fire escape. (This is definitely something to think

sidered sex, drugs and rock-n-roll an important way of life. She would walk by me, as I sipped from a delightful, frosty can of Budweiser, and shake her head in dismay. Then, she would go into her bedroom and throw things and yell.

When her behavior became unbearable, I told her to move out, and this she told me, was "the most horrible thing" anyone had ever done to her. She pretended to look for an apartment for two months, and when I finally realized that she wasn't actually looking at all, I was forced to give her an ultimatum of one more month of rent-stabilized bliss, after which, she finally packed up her Melissa Ethridge records and got the Hell out.

My new roommate is never home. He pays his rent, but I have only seen him twice. He goes to the bodega and comes back five days later. This is the perfect roommate. I also have a new, four-legged roommate — a one and a half pound Chihuahua named Reverend Jen Junior who was born with elf ears and who sleeps on my head at night. This is also an example of a perfect roommate.

I'm sorry if this chapter, which was supposed to be about living on the Lower East Side has become a rant about roommates, but as you'll find upon talking with many LES-dwellers, roommates are an important part of life on the LES. The walls here are paper thin, allowing you to comprehensively study the sexual fetishes of everyone in your building. The notion of privacy is long forgotten in this hood.

If you do have an affinity for bizarre (and loud) sexual fetishes it is important that your roommate be well aware of this, and that they don't judge you too harshly. This is why I strongly recommend an extensive screening of all prospective

Helpful hint: If attacked by a roommate, with whom you share a lease, DO NOT fight back, unless you truly believe that your life is in danger. Rather, accept the pain, and know that in the end, you will be the victor. Do, however, get a restraining order.

My second roommate was OK, until she decided to become an actress and began studying the "Meisner" technique. This involved her working several thousand hours a week in order to pay for her acting classes, which meant that she lost any sense of humor she once had, and it also meant that she and her acting partner spent most of their time torturing me by doing "repetition" exercises in the kitchen. Repetition exercises are like the adult equivalent of the "I know you are, but what am I?" game. Meisner also encourages neophyte actors to "get in touch" with their emotions. Often, Roommate #2 got in touch with her anger by hurling furniture in her bedroom.

When Roommate #2 finally landed an agent, he told her she was too heavy and encouraged her to lose weight. For some reason, she also decided that this would be a good time to stop smoking and drinking. All at once, she gave up smoking, drinking and eating, and she began to exercise every morning. In short, she became an asshole. She became angry with me for having friends over who smoked, and demanded that they venture into our heinously dank hallway in order to smoke, despite the fact that she had only quit for a month. (I was happy to see, only a month ago, that she had taken up smoking again! It's the self-righteous ones who never last!)

Because Roommate #2 gave up all vice (except for her closeted lesbian affair—but you didn't hear it from me!) she became extremely judgmental of anyone who still con-

Photo: Monica Mohan

are much different than that of tourists. "How'd you like the tour?" I ask.

"It was great—just like visiting my apartment," they say.

This is true. The actual structures themselves have barely changed. My own apartment is a shining example of this. They are still cramped and rarely have closets or doors. My apartment has no closets, and my bedroom didn't have a door for quite some time. (Until I convinced an ex-boyfriend to install one for me.) Actually, at one time, my bedroom did have a door, but when I threw one of my psychotic roommates out, she chose to vindictively take my door with her.

Due to the cramped living conditions on the Lower East Side, I would suggest that if you do decide to live here, that you adore and trust whoever it is that you choose to live with. Of course, this can always backfire because the stress of living in the city is so great, and it is so tough to make it here, that many a sane person has gone insane from the pressure. (Think of Ginsburg's *Howl*.)

My first Lower East Side roommate seemed like a nice girl when she first moved in with me, but I watched her slowly start to crack. One day, she came home with a stick of dynamite tattooed on her arm, and I knew it was all over for me. A month later she came home with a belly piercing and a giant tattoo of a Chinese symbol on her back, which for all she knew probably translated meant, "jackass." Because of the tattoo on her back and the piercing on her stomach, she could only lie on her side, and this made her quite irritable, so much so that one day, while enraged over my having imbibed her Pepsi, she grabbed a handful of my hair, and slammed my head into a cement wall several times while uttering threats that she would indeed kill me.

Despite the fact that I'm sure this incident left me with irreparable brain damage, it also left me with the lease to a rent-stabilized apartment in Downtown Manhattan, and for that, I am extremely grateful.

The gentrification of the LES has affected my well being in several ways. For starters, my new neighbors tend to blare techno out of their expensive stereo equipment into my oversized listeners at all hours of the day and night. This, coupled with my severe insomnia, means that I have slept a total of four hours this year. I have attempted to don earplugs (which I enjoy anyway, since they feel a bit like *Q-tips*) and to place a pillow over my head, but it is all for naught. Nothing can deflect the booming bass of my ghastly neighbors.

Five years ago, no one in this building could have afforded such a fine stereo. Gentrification is not just pushing out small businesses and raising rents—it's ruining my sleeping patterns! If you don't believe that gentrification is sweeping the Lower East Side, I welcome you to visit my building, where, while ascending the stairs, you can hear rats screeching out of one ear, and out of the other, you can hear neighbors discuss different shades of Chanel lipstick.

Recently, I got a job working at the visitor's center of the Lower East Side Tenement Museum, a historic landmark located at 97 Orchard Street. At the Tenement Museum visitors have an opportunity to visit a tenement building, which was built in 1864, where they learn about the lives of different immigrants at the turn of the century. While life on the Lower East Side was extremely difficult in the 1800's, I am often shocked to hear the reactions of tourists to the tour. "I don't know how they lived without air conditioning!" they often say. But, no one I know in this neighborhood has air conditioning. The people I do know, who have it, use it as a ploy to seduce other, less fortunate residents of the neighborhood, during heat waves.

What many of the tourists don't realize is that apartments, which are very similar to the ones in the Tenement Museum are being rented out for $2,000 dollars a month by unscrupulous landlords.

The reactions of friends to the Tenement Museum tour

Chapter Four
Living on the Lower East Side

Since my emancipation from the Salvation Army Women's Residence, I have lived in many neighborhoods in New York City, including The Upper West Side, Midtown, and Williamsburg (No, not Colonial Williamsburg, but Williamsburg, Brooklyn, an extremely trendy "annex" to the Lower East Side. If one were to liken the Lower East Side to the Brady's home on *The Brady Bunch*, Williamsburg would be the equivalent of Greg Brady's attic / bedroom.) I have even lived in Jersey City, and I can assure you that the Lower East Side is the greatest neighborhood in all the land. Although, I am fearful that it will not remain this way for long. You see New York City is becoming rapidly gentrified, and the poor people like me are being driven out.[7] One could almost liken artists to rats, and real estate developers and landlords to the Pied Piper. (I like rats so this is not a slur.) Soon, New York City (the Lower East Side included) will become a residence for people with well-manicured nails, well-coifed hairdos and health insurance.

Eight years ago, when I moved to the LES, I used to get the creeps whenever I'd walk down Ludlow Street late at night and hear carnival-type music filtering out onto the street, and see hobgoblin-looking drunks weaving down the sidewalk. Now all the drunks are good-looking. Luckily though, the drinking hasn't subsided. In fact, drinking has increased, and we will discuss this at length in Chapter Five. However, being a natural adventure-seeker (or masochist) I miss the fear of traipsing around dangerous streets at ungodly hours.

FOR THE LOVE OF GOD: SHUT UP!
DUDE, THIS NEW MOBY CD ROCKS!
TOTALLY!

Hyou-stun

How-stun

totally un-sexy because of their level of superficiality. SOHO is also a good place to go if you want to drink eight-dollar beers, and get treated like shit.

Once, I tried to go to a bar called "Spy" in SOHO, and the doorperson wouldn't let me in because he said (this is an exact quote) "You look like a freak!" (I was wearing my elf ears at the time.) SOHO used to have the redeeming quality of being home to a number of art galleries, but the rents got so high, that gallery owners said, "Fuck it!" And, they moved to Chelsea, which sucks because there is nowhere to pee in Chelsea. At least in SOHO there were bars and restaurants where you could use the bathroom. Now, going to galleries means not drinking any liquids beforehand. I never thought I'd see the day when viewing art equaled dehydration.

Chelsea is the neighborhood above the West Village, which is the neighborhood directly above SOHO.

But, this isn't a book about Chelsea or any of those other neighborhoods. In fact, this isn't really a book about the Lower East Side. It's a book about how to enjoy yourself and about how to make the most of your journey to the Lower East Side. If I wanted to write a book about the Lower East Side, I would have to do a lot of research on the history of the Lower East Side, and I simply don't have time. For instance, I have heard that Houston Street is named after some dude whose last name was "Houston" and that he liked it to be pronounced "How-Stun." But, I don't know what this dude did to have a street named after him, and quite frankly, I don't care, and I don't think you care either.

You care about where to go in order to have fun, drink, meet hot people and eat pizza.

I'll leave the history part up to the historians, and they can leave the fun part up to me.

Chapter Three
Houston Street

First things first: Houston Street is pronounced "How-Stun" Street, not "Hyou-Stun" Street (like Houston, Texas). If you do pronounce it "Hyou-Stun" everyone will know you're a dork.

Houston Street is a big street, which separates the Lower East Side from the rest of the world. Houston Street runs East / West, not North / South.

The neighborhood above Houston Street on the East Side is the East Village. Sometimes, people refer to the East Village as "the Lower East Side." They do this because both neighborhoods are cool and edgy and filled with people who either do heroin or look like they do heroin, and because, long ago, the East Village was also considered "the Lower East Side" until realtors decided to start calling it the "East Village" to make it seem more marketable like the West Village. You might also hear the East Village referred to as "Loisada" a name, which it gets from its large Latino community.

The neighborhood directly below Houston Street on the West Side is SOHO. SOHO stands for "South Of Houston Street." My friend, Lorne, once told me that he was walking home from a bar in SOHO one evening, with our friend Robert. Apparently, he asked Robert, "Where exactly is the line between SOHO and the Lower East Side?" And, at that exact moment, a giant rat traipsed in front of them, and Lorne said, "Oh! I guess that's it!"

You know you've left SOHO and arrived on the Lower East Side when an obese rat crosses your path.

SOHO is filled with absurdly attractive people who are

a millionaire, but the truth is, I am good at many things, but what I am best at is making no money. I do a lot of things for free, and it's partly because I am altruistic and love art, and it's partly because I am stupid. One thing is certain, when I win the 45 million dollar lotto jackpot, I won't be one of those people who don't know how to spend that much money, and so it ruins their life. Forty-five million dollars would vastly improve the quality of my life, and I would know exactly how to spend it.

hot fudge sundae all over myself at the local Dairy Queen.

When I got to high school, I no longer resembled Meatloaf, but I was still tormented due to my visionary ideas, and unwillingness to "put out." When I was 16 the cool kids in my high school painted the phrase "You Are a Art Fag" on the street in front of my home. (I knew it was the cool kids because of the grammatical error. It should have been "*an*" art fag.) Because the street was city property, it was graveled over by city workers.

That is when I knew I had to come to New York.

I am 29 years old. By the time you read this, I will probably be 30 years old. A lot of my buds say, "Man, when I was a kid, I thought 30 seemed so old. I thought I would have a house, a car, a couple of kids, a job, health insurance and a 401K Plan." I never thought I would have a house, a car, kids, a job or a 401K Plan. In fact, I don't even know what a 401K Plan is. I somehow knew I would end up here—sweating in my un-air-conditioned, sixth-floor-walk-up, tenement apartment, waiting for my friend, Faceboy, to come over, so we can carry giant, *papier-mâché* mushrooms over to the theater where I will be performing my play, *Lord of the Cockrings* to a group of twelve drunk audience members who will heckle us, and perhaps hurl empty beer cans at the stage.

Despite the less than stellar turnout at many of my shows, it could be said that I have become marginally famous (meaning a lot of people in Downtown Manhattan and Williamsburg recognize me, but no one, anywhere else in the country or world does) for undertaking many ambitious art projects including my pioneering of Hal, the religion of the uncool, and my opening of the world's only troll museum in my apartment. I am also the entrepreneur behind www.revjen.com as well as the author of several self-published books and the host of Reverend Jen's Anti-Slam, the longest running open mike on Ludlow Street.

You might be thinking that with all of my projects, I am

Photo: Monica Mohan

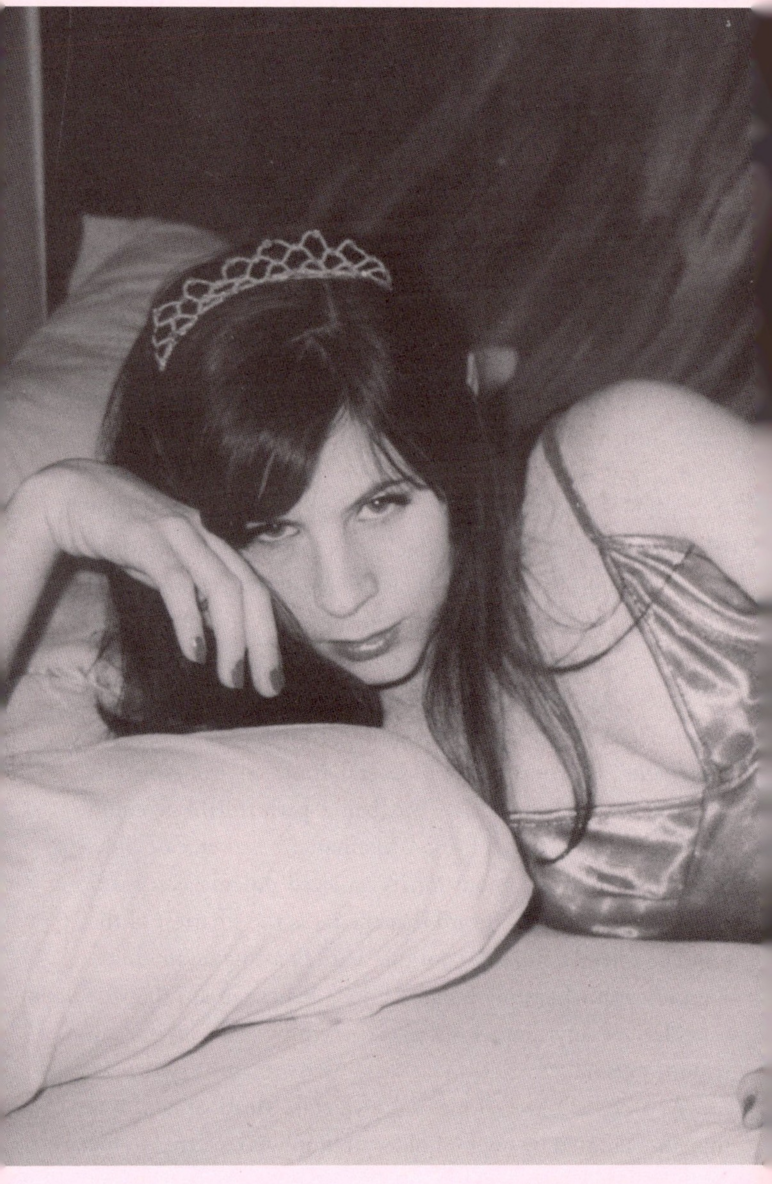

Chapter Two
Meet Your Guide!

Before we begin our tour, I think it's important that you get to know me. My name is Saint Reverend Jen. I am a poet, preacher, painter, performer, prophet, literary giant, upcoming celebrity/personality, lady wrestler, troll museum curator, ear wax-removal specialist, Patron Saint of the Uncool and Voice of the Downtrodden and Tired. I was born on July 24th, 1972. Amelia Aerhart was born on July 24th and so was Lord Dunsany (author of *The King of Elfland's Daughter*.) According to my personal astrologer, Jackie Stallone, this makes me a "Leo Type 3" which is perhaps, the most ambitious sign in the entire zodiac. This also means I was born during the Nixon administration, and during the "year of the rat" which could explain a great number of things, including my affinity with rodents. (A couple of years ago, I penned a musical entitled *Rats* which appears in my first book, *Sex Symbol for the Insane*. I performed *Rats* several times in front of The Winter Garden where *Cats* was being performed.) It could also explain why I now live on Manhattan's Lower East Side, a neighborhood as famous for its cat-sized rodents as it is for its knishes. I have also heard that the rat is the smartest of the Chinese calendar animals, not that I am boasting or anything. I am not really boasting because I don't believe in astrology or calendars or anything. I am an "everything happens for no reason" person.

As a child, I looked like the rock star, Meatloaf, and was therefore taunted by my four older siblings who referred to me as "Fat-Head" and "Sweathog." For a couple of years in my early adolescence I was called "Dairy Queen" after I spilled a

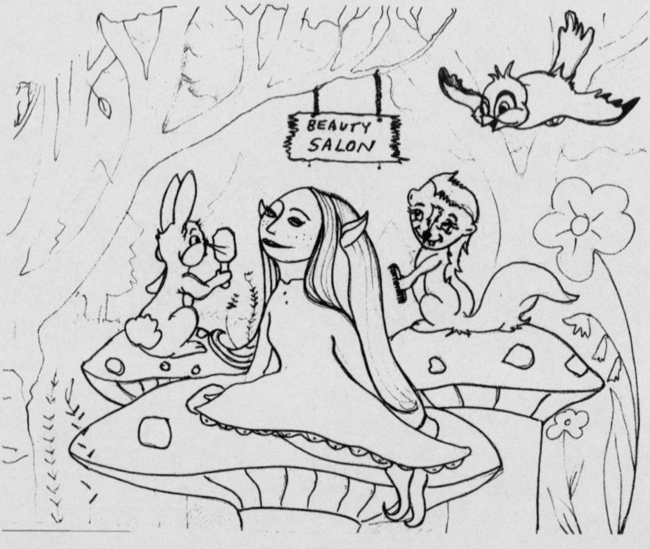
BEAUTY
SALON

this trip through the several circles of the Lower East Side. Now, close your eyes, and imagine that you are on top of a double-decker bus, freezing your ass off, and that I am speaking loudly into a microphone in the seat next to you. Put on your seatbelt! It is going to be a wild ride!!!

5. I don't mean to insinuate that we were cool in anyway by alluding to our drug use. A gap-toothed hippie named "Cloud" for whom I'd written a term paper gave my first hits of acid to me. Mostly, Julia and I just did our homework while tripping. We also enjoyed "dumpster diving" while tripping where in we would find cool objects to make art out of. On one occasion, we found a retro, 1960's Electrolux Vacuum, which we attempted to drag home from the Bowery. Eventually, we stopped and took a break at Continental, parking the Electrolux outside while we had a quick drink inside. When we came out, not more than a half hour later, the hose on the Electrolux had vanished! This was my first inkling that New York is a town full of perverse individuals.

6. I like to think that if it hadn't been for my love affair with Dog, I would have gone on to become a "functioning" member of society, but the truth is that it is probably impossible for me to function in any capacity other than "art star." Also, the fact that I became an art star rather than a soccer mom isn't necessarily a good thing, except for maybe the fact that I would make an unfit parent, but I make a fit artist. (Not physically fit mind you.)

"famous artist." I mean an incredibly talented artist who was also a non-conformist misfit. There were plenty of conformist misfits. They all wore black and listened to Joy Division. Dog P. was different. He wore handmade helmets with trolls and horns attached to them, and had a shrine to Jim Henson in his apartment. He worshipped the number 12, and had developed 12 types of dances, each named after a different type of cheese, which he had no qualms about doing at the hippest parties, from which we would immediately be alienated. He helped me see that New York is a place of limitless opportunities for fun and mayhem, and he made me realize that the best way to see New York is through the eyes of someone slightly mad.

I therefore would consider it an honor if you, the reader, would allow me to be the slightly mad Virgil to your Dante in

wanted to go to a normal college.

I was planning on leaving New York at the end of my second semester, when a dramatic change of events occurred. I fell in love.

He appeared at the only party I'd been invited to that year. His name was "Dog P." and he had long, flowing dirty-blonde hair and a handlebar moustache. He was sporting skintight powder blue slacks and a polyester ivory, blue and brown shirt with the top three buttons left undone so as to reveal his ample chest hair. He looked like Jesus circa 1976. Even though I'd never really even had a boyfriend, I knew right away I was in love.

We went into his bedroom, smoked a joint, closed the door, took off our clothes and "did it." It was amazing. We lay in bed, holding each other. However, the pot mixed with the gallons of booze suddenly made me nauseous, so much so that I leaned over and vomited in a cup next to his bed.

This did not alter the course of our romance and I spent the next six years of my life with him. Had this drug-induced act of love not occurred, I most certainly would have transferred schools, and probably would have ended up a soccer mom slicing oranges rather than an art star offering up insightful travel guides.[6]

I am therefore extremely grateful to Dog P. for altering the course of my life, and perhaps the course of art history, as we know it.

Dog P. was the type of person I'd hoped to meet in New York. He was an art star. And by "art star" I don't mean

Salvation Army would allow, and walked over to their table. "Hallo. My name is Jen." I said. They looked at me like I'd sprouted a third arm out of my forehead, and this is when I realized that the absolute freakiest thing you can do in New York is be friendly.

Both Julia and Kim were a bit standoffish, and I wasn't sure I liked them, but I was desperate. If Charlie Manson had walked into the cafeteria in drag, I probably would've tried to befriend him. Julia let me know almost immediately that her last name "de Groat" meant "the Great" in Dutch. She had been a total art star in her neighborhood in Upstate, and I realized that she would have a difficult time. I'd been lucky enough to have a teacher who hurled paintings across the classroom if he thought they sucked. I didn't think I was great, and my name was totally boring. I was like, "My name is Jennifer. It means I was born in the '70s."

But Julia and I had a lot in common. We loved painting, punk rock and Jack Kerouac, and we were anxious to delve into the seedy underbelly of New York's subculture. Kim I got along with, but she was just like all the other Phil Collins lovers I'd met. Julia became my first friend in New York.

Together, Julia and I discovered clubs like CBGB and Continental (which was my fave place back then because they served me booze despite the fact that I looked 12 and had no ID). We also discovered LSD, which helped me realize there was a lot more to New York than meets the naked eye.[5]

Julia and I both wanted to meet boys. She responded to a personals ad in *The Village Voice*, and met a hot Latino boy named Sam. They started fucking (at his place, obviously) and I was once again, totally alone. Julia spent all of her time conjuring up ways to try to sneak Sam into our apartment, but it was all for naught. I occupied my time being the biggest art nerd that ever lived.

I was so depressed. I wanted to leave New York. I called my parents and told them I wanted to transfer schools. I

I tried to call my friends in Maryland, but they were all out partying at University of Maryland keggers.

I sat at my desk in my four-foot-gnome-cave apartment, and drew constantly. This was my first inkling that life as a visionary would be lonely. It seemed that most of the women at The Parkside were absolute miscreants. Whatever feminist coined the phrase "a woman without a man is like a fish without a bicycle," never visited The Parkside. I had been told that The Parkside was a residence for young women, but I found many of the residents there to be elderly women who had lived there since they were young women, and who had, since that time, developed romantic liaisons with other formerly young, now elderly residents, which equaled soft-core elderly porn in the cafeteria and elevators—and we're not talking about elderly lipstick lesbians. We're talking seventy-five year old women with bowl haircuts, tongueing each other in the lobby.

After a couple of days of getting settled in, my classes started. I was a painting/fine arts major (because I'm always thinking about the future) but my first year, I was forced to take the same foundation courses as the graphic designers and illustrators. I remember expecting other art students to be free-spirited bohemians like myself. Much to my horror, I discovered that most of my classmates listened to Phil Collins and longed to someday work in advertising. I tried to make friends, but most of my classmates regarded me as a freak who was overzealous about making art.

I wanted to make friends so badly, but every day The Parkside cafeteria, where my two daily meals were served, was filled with either elderly women in mumus, or young women in purple sweatpants, sweatshirts and pumps, who looked at me like I was the freak. Then one day I was shocked and delighted to see two hip looking chicks who appeared to be college students. One had long, blonde hair and tan skin. The other had long, black hair and pasty skin. I decided to "try to make friends." I filled my tray with the limited goods that the

Chapter One
Entering the Land of Make Believe

I moved to New York City in 1990 in order to attend The School of Visual Arts. Because SVA didn't have traditional student housing, I took a room at The Parkside Evangeline, a Salvation Army-run residence on Gramercy Park South. The Parkside had been recommended by Zoe, a student advisor who'd taken my parents and me out for coffee and pastries, which, looking back, I'm sure were laced with drugs.

If you overlooked the fact that The Parkside had the exterior of a 1940's Mental Institution where lobotomies were being cranked out and the interior of a convent, it was an attractive building. My room was tiny, yet clean. It came with a desk, a bed and a closet, and that's all that there was room for. I had not yet honed my decorating skills, nor had I transported my massive troll collection from Maryland, so my only decorations were a Ramones poster, a purple bedspread, and a replica of a shrunken head, which I found comforting.

It was my first time being away from Maryland for an extended period of time. I didn't know a single person in New York. I had not one friend, and to top it all off, The Parkside was an all-female residence! It was just like Bosom Buddies, only there was no Tom Hanks or other guy to keep me company, while I poured over my homework—just me, my Ramones poster and my shrunken head.

I told myself that I wasn't there to make friends, I was there to become the greatest art star of the upcoming millennium, but after three days I was desperately lonely and horny.

frankly, I have had it up to here with these harbingers of doom. I am tired of hearing people bemoan the fact that, "New York sucks now." New York may not be as cool as it once was, or as cheap as it once was, and the Lower East Side may not be as edgy as it once was, but it is still a home to misfits worldwide, and that is why I write this travel guide, a guide full of contradictions, self-indulgence, nonsense and hope.

---

1. The abuse that was heaped upon me during my adolescence in Maryland is detailed in my upcoming autobiography; *People Who Don't Like My Work are Bad People*, which will be available nowhere very soon.

2. Although Giuliani took credit for "making the city safer," the drop in crime swept across the entirety of America and could be attributed as much to the switch in taste from crack to heroin in the early nineties as it could to Giuliani's Gestapo tactics.

3. Except in Mexico and England.

4. Movements which first gained strength on the LES have greatly affected the face of America at large, namely the Labor movement and housing reform. It is therefore not too implausible to imagine that a group of dysfunctional art stars might affect the rest of the country through their actions.

for fat Oregonians. I am torn. On the one hand, America could have said, "Fuck New York. Let those freaks clean up their own goddamn mess," and we New Yorkers would have been financially screwed more than we already are. Tourism would have stopped. I would be out of a job again. It is because of the Oregonians in their buttons that many businesses stayed afloat.

On the other hand, this seemed like the perfect opportunity for New York City to secede from America. But, more and more, it seems like America is engulfing New York. It is no longer possible to obtain a forty dollar blow-job in Times Square, but it is possible to obtain a forty dollar Donald Duck sweatshirt. Don't get me wrong. I am not of the mind that we should all stop shopping and consuming. This book is pretty much all about consuming. But, I think that there needs to be more variety on the menu. We should be able to buy forty-dollar blowjobs and sweatshirts! I have heard several people utter the phrase, "Yeah, I mean Giuliani's sort of a dick, but he did make the city safer."[2] What they forget is that safer also means more expensive, and I'd rather dodge bullets on my way home from a one-hour day at work, than walk safely home from an eight-hour day at work.

By the time you get your paws on this book it is quite possible that many of the places I mention in the following pages will no longer exist. For instance, had I written this book in 1995, I would have devoted several pages to Woolworth's, which is now an enterprise of the past.[3] It is therefore important that readers approach this manuscript as a historical document as well as a travel guide.

Despite this, I feel quite certain that no matter how many Disney realtors and Duane Reades lay claim to this land, there will always be a diverse group of people searching for hope here, and there will always be a small group of bohemians enjoying themselves below 14th Street, and quite possibly affecting the world at large through their ideas.[4] And, quite

D.C. would simply be impotent, but New York is just right. That is why I continue to work excessively degrading jobs (giant frog at the zoo, Christmas elf at Bloomingdales, security guard at the Met…) in order to continue to pay my landlord the entirety of my paltry pay for the privilege of living here, in squalor.

When I do visit my older siblings in Maryland, I am often overwhelmed by the luxury of their living environment. They have couches, tables, utensils and cars. Their sink and toilet are in the same room, and they have hot water! But my jealous awe usually subsides when I realize that they don't have open mikes or dildo stores right around the corner. There is a lot to be said for comfort, but there is also a lot to be said for being able to obtain a butt-plug, a six-pack of Budweiser and a psychic reading on one block.

September 11th changed the way America saw New York, and it changed the way New Yorkers viewed their living situation and their city. Suddenly, an adulterous Mayor who'd spent 8 years fighting squeegee guys, pretzel vendors, titty bars, club kids and poop-paintings was a wartime hero. I realize it is unpopular to criticize politicians during this time, but he was an asshole, and he is still an asshole. In fact, most New Yorkers who were once assholes are still assholes, and yet tourists from Oregon voyaged to New York in busloads, proudly adorned with "Oregon Loves New York" buttons. Suddenly, the tank-top sporting, macho metropolis was a pity fuck

In less than an hour, complete and total chaos overtook the city, and people were terrified. For months, people were terrified. In my conscious state, I would think, "I'm not scared. Everything's going to be OK." But then I would go to sleep and be confronted by nightmares in which buildings collapsed and people shrieked. The sound of trucks driving across the Williamsburg Bridge was enough to make me jump fifty feet out of my chair. But at no time did I ever consider leaving this city. It never even occurred to me that I could move somewhere else.

Shortly after the attack, the *New York Times Magazine* featured an article about terrified yuppies who were fleeing to the suburbs. I spoke to friends, who were already making plans to move to L.A. (Most of them moved back.) And, I didn't understand. I would rather stay right here in Downtown Manhattan and serve as a living target for religious fundamentalists than move back to the suburbs of Maryland where I was ostracized for 17 years.[1] I am either a slave to New York, a masochist or a freak who can't live anywhere else because no other city will have me. No other city has embraced me like New York, and no other city has destroyed me like New York. I suffer from Battered Wife Syndrome and New York is my tank-top-sporting, face-slapping, well-hung husband. If each city in the world had a penis, New York's would be the biggest, the most orgasm-inducing, hardest member of them all, and this is why I continue to live here. L.A. would have a drippy penis. Chicago would have a cold clammy penis and

cynical moments, I cannot lose faith in New York. I am sure a more logical person who is more interested in selling twelve million copies of her book would probably decide to not continue writing a travel guide for a city where tourism has declined significantly, but I am not a logical person. No one who lives in New York City is logical. We pay exorbitant rents in order to live in shoeboxes in a city that smells like ass. However, New York offers something which other cities often fail to provide, and that is a sense of belonging. I moved to New York thirteen years ago from Maryland, and within a year, I considered myself a New Yorker. It was in my blood. One cannot go to L.A. and suddenly become an L.A.-er. They don't even have a word for it there! But, what exactly is a New Yorker? The answer is there's no correct answer. The face of New York is as diverse as the face of America. (Although with a lot fewer obese people.) And, that is part of its beauty.

I started writing this travel guide in August of 2001. I'd only completed the first chapter, when the September 11th attack on the World Trade Center occurred. I was fortunate in that all of my loved ones went physically unscathed (except for the soap-sized bars of asbestos, which I'm sure we all inhaled), but like most New Yorkers, I was mentally devastated. The explosion that Tuesday woke me up. I looked out my bedroom window, expecting to see a tenement building collapsing as they often do, or even thinking that maybe my own building had started to collapse, and saw people staring toward Delancey Street, their mouths agape in horror. I ran to my kitchen window and saw that both towers had holes in them and were on fire. I thought the city had been bombed, as I have half expected it to be for some time now. I was waiting for more bombs to fall, and thought that I was going to die in a few moments, tending as I do to always jump to the most heinous conclusions possible. All of my usual existential / suicidal feelings fled from my being and I was grasped by an overwhelming desire to live, yet felt totally powerless.

was he coming from? He seemed too happy to be coming from a job. It seemed to me that being Mr. Rogers was his job. Even the others in the neighborhood seemed jobless, like "Lady Aberlin." I looked her up on the web to see if she actually had a job, and all it said was, "She is a caring friend to the puppets and neighbors of Make Believe." That's it. That was her job. Even the others, who had occupations, like chef or mailman, obviously didn't work full time because they spent so much goddamn time shooting the shit with Mr. Rogers. They were grownups who spent their days hanging out and talking to puppets. The people in Mr. Rogers' neighborhood were like the characters in Warhol's factory sans the drugs and glamour.

I suppose *Mr. Rogers' Neighborhood* left a lasting impression on me in that it made me search for such an unconventional neighborhood when I grew up—a place where I could live and talk to puppets and be praised for it. I like to think of myself as the Fred Rogers of the Lower East Side in that I talk to my puppets and trolls whenever I get the chance, and I entertain other jobless, talented entities as often as possible. The only difference between Fred and me is that I still have to work a couple days a week, and I like to drink beer when my friends come over.

But, there is more to me writing this travel companion than an attempt to take over as the Fred Rogers of the new millennium. The simple act of writing this book at this time defies all logic and any notion of what a "publishable book" is. Had I gone to a literary agent and said, "Look, I want to write a travel guide for Downtown Manhattan," they would have laughed in my face. In fact, only a couple of weeks ago, at my friend Faceboy's open mike, a psychic took the stage, and made the pronouncement that in five years, Manhattan would no longer exist. Perhaps I should have heeded the words of this Downtown Nostradaumus and stopped writing a travel guide for a city that it seems might collapse, but even in my most

An Introduction

When word began to spread that I'd put pen to paper in order to write a travel guide to the Lower East Side, a lot of people asked me, "Why the fuck are you writing a travel guide, Reverend Jen? For starters, you can't afford to go anywhere. You consider getting a rollini instead of a slice an extravagant meal, and you only shop at the Salvation Army. Not only that, while it seems to most people that you live in an apartment on the Lower East Side, the truth is that you live in your own screwed-up head, which is very far from the Lower East Side or from any civilized place on Earth. How can you tell other people where to go and what to do?"

These folks are right. I am too poor to go anywhere or do anything. The last movie I saw in the theater was probably *Titanic*, and I can really only judge most restaurants by the way they smell from outside on the sidewalk. Not to mention, I do live in my own world, a world where residing in a troll museum and donning plastic elf ears is acceptable.

But, why is it that all travel guides must be written by academic types? What about travel guides written by social deviants and freaks? They are bound to offer better suggestions on how to spend one's time. And, to be honest, this isn't even so much a travel guide as it is an attempt to mask my disorganized mess of essays and ramblings as a "useful" book, which is vaguely about the neighborhood in which I live—a really cool neighborhood, no doubt. As a child, one of the things I liked about the TV show, *Mr. Rogers' Neighborhood*, was the fact that Mr. Rogers seemed to have a really fun life. Did he have a job? I don't remember him ever mentioning it. When he came home, and changed into his sweater, where

Photo: Maurice Narcis

The Rest of the World

on Street
HOT BAGELS   KATZ'S

Street
AMUNDI

THE "HAT"
GRILLED CHEESE

Ludlow Street

Street

ey Street

Essex Street

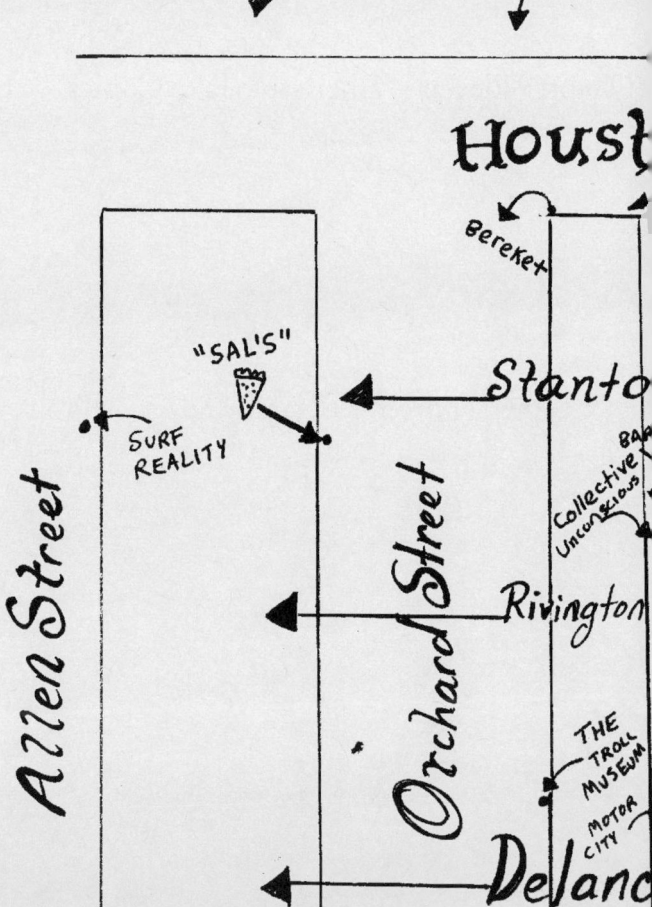

The Lower East Side

Houst[on]
- Bereket
- "SAL'S"
- SURF REALITY
- Stanto[n]
- Collective Unconscious / BAR
- Rivington
- THE TROLL MUSEUM
- MOTOR CITY
- Delan[cey]

Allen Street • Orchard Street

Chapter Eight : Reverend Jen's Lower East Side Troll Museum   87

Chapter Nine : Open Mikes   93

Chapter Eleven : Where to Make Copies   107

Chapter Thirteen : Delancey Street   113

Chapter Sixteen : What the Future Holds   131

Chapter Six : Pizza   75

Chapter Seven : Love Connections   83

Chapter Ten : Mexican Food   103

Chapter Twelve : Where To Get Porn
                  and Other Potentially Embarrassing Stuff   109

Chapter Fourteen : Food Court   119

Chapter Fifteen : Miscellaneous   125

Contents

Introduction 11

Chapter One : Entering the Land of Make Believe 19

Chapter Two : Meet Your Guide! 27

Chapter Three : Houston Street 33

Chapter Four : Living on the Lower East Side 37

Chapter Five : Drinking 47

For Reverend Jen Junior

Reverend Jen's Really Cool Neighborhood / Les Misrahi
by Saint Reverend Jen
© 2003 Saint Reverend Jen & Printed Matter, Inc.

All rights reserved. No part of this book may be reproduced or translated in any form or by any means, in whole or in part, without prior written permission from the publisher and artist / author.

Published in the United States of America in 2003 by Printed Matter, Inc.
535 West 22nd Street, New York, NY 10011
Telephone: 212 925-0325, Fax: 212 925-0464
Website: http://www.printedmatter.org

ISBN: 0-89439-011-2

Designed by Garrick Gott.
Cover Photos by Maurice Narcis.
All pictures and illustrations by Saint Reverend Jen unless otherwise noted.

Reverend Jen's Really Cool Neighborhood / Les Misrahi is an original book by Saint Reverend Jen published by Printed Matter, Inc.

Printed Matter's Publishing Program for Emerging Artists was made possible through generous support of New York City's Department of Cultural Affairs. Additional support has also been provided by The Andy Warhol Foundation for the Arts, the Elizabeth Firestone Graham Foundation, and the Heyday Foundation.

Printed Matter, Inc. is an independent 501(c)(3) non-profit organization founded in 1976 by artists and art workers with the mission to foster the appreciation, dissemination, and understanding of artists' books and other artists' publications.

Printed Matter, Inc. is not affiliated with, nor a division of, any other non-profit organization.

Printed and bound in Canada.

74289A
$14.95

Reverend Jen's
Really Cool Neighborhood

Printed Matter, Inc.